Spirituality of Hope

SEGUNDO GALILEA

Spirituality of Hope

Translated from the Spanish
by Terrence Cambias

ORBIS BOOKS

Maryknoll, New York 10545

The Catholic Foreign Mission Society of America (Maryknoll) recruits and trains people for overseas missionary service. Through Orbis Books, Maryknoll aims to foster the international dialogue that is essential to mission. The books published, however, reflect the opinions of their authors and are not meant to represent the official position of the society.

Manuscript Editor: William E. Jerman

ISBN 0-88344-636-7

Table of Contents

Introduction

The Bible and the faith of the church tell us that God is Trinity. The Trinity is accepted and lived in Christian spirituality. But not all Christians are equally conscious of the role that each one of the three Persons of the Trinity plays in their lives. Christians can usually say something about God the Father and Jesus Christ the Son. But they have less to say about the Holy Spirit, although they know the Holy Spirit is God, and that Holy Spirit is important in their lives. For many the Holy Spirit is the most "confusing" person of the Trinity.

In a similar way the Bible and the faith of the Church tell us that we can unite ourselves with the Trinity through the three theological virtues, faith, hope, and charity—the three spiritual faculties that God gives to humankind to breach the infinite gap between Creator and creature. Through these virtues we can experience God here on earth. Mystical theology teaches us that faith and hope are inseparable, that if one grows, the other grows with it, and if one decreases, so does the other. It also teaches us that charity is the greatest of the three, to the point that it alone will remain in the definitive encounter with God in eternity. Love by itself is sufficient to identify us with a God who is Love. But faith and hope on earth are as necessary as charity to experience the love of God. God is given to us here in a way that is "limited, and as in a mirror." We need to believe in and hope for God in order to love God (1 Cor. 13).

If we asked Christians to explain their faith, hope, and charity, many would have a good deal to say about charity, somewhat less about faith, and very little about hope, even though they live it implicitly.

Hope—Christian hope, the second theological virtue—has become central to the language of God's people. Latin America is called the continent of hope. There the poor and marginated bear witness to hope. We are told that we should deepen a spirituality of hope, that the world today, terrorized and frustrated, needs to hear the Good News of hope. But hope remains for many a vague virtue. Believers of good will understand the content of hope in different ways.

For some, hope means realizing legitimate personal, familial, and social hopes and desires. For others it means achieving relief for those who suffer, justice for the poor, liberation for the oppressed—the hope for a better society. Still others see hope as a happier future, the solution to their own and the world's more serious problems.

Is all this Christian hope? Is it even a part of Christian hope? How is Christian hope distinguished from idealism? Could not the language of hope be secularized, as happens with the language of faith and charity? There is nothing easier to distort than charity. Being gratified or feeling productive easily take the place of forgetting self for the sake of God and other persons. It is also easy to replace faith in God's revelation with human faith in persons, ideologies, or projects. If that happens, hope, inseparable from faith and condemned to frustration without charity, would also be replaced by human hopes.

At the same time, if Christian hope loses its content, it will eventually empty faith and charity of theirs. The theological virtues, whose content is the full experience of God and neighbor, would be transformed into mere experiences of human progress.

For the Christian scriptures the authenticity of faith, hope, and charity is the very basis of Christian identity. The most profound pages in scripture are about the theological virtues. Particularly relevant are the syntheses on faith in the Epistle to the Hebrews (11:1–40: "Faith is confident assurance concerning what we hope for, and conviction about things we do not see"); and on charity in the First Epistle to the Corinthians (13:1–13:

"If I have faith great enough to move mountains, but have not love, I am nothing"). Hope is also amply treated in the Christian scriptures, either together with faith, or more explicitly, responding to the persecuted early Christian communities' need for hope. Thus the Apocalypse is a prophecy about Christian hope in times of tribulation and martyrdom. The epistles of St. Peter continually deal with the believer as a person of hope, and with the motives and content of Christian hope. "Should anyone ask you the reason for this hope of yours, be ever ready to reply" (1 Pet. 3:15).

The Christian gives reasons for hope in a world that has no hope. The Christian can provide the key to a change of heart from hopelessness and resignation to the hope that builds the future of humankind.

The following pages seek to contribute so that we Christians give reasons for the hope we received in baptism—a hope destined to grow like "a fountain . . . leaping up to provide eternal life" (John 4:14). This is not a work of theological research nor is it systematically elaborated. It is a collection of reflections to inspire the mystique of Christian hope, an integral part of the spirituality so necessary today for our personal lives. Christian hope is especially necessary today as part of the content of evangelization.

1

What Hope Is, and What It Is Not

The president of a country heavily in debt and with a seriously deteriorated economy announces in a speech that the situation has to improve and that the next few years will be better, with strong economic development. "We are moving forward; the future is ours. I ask of all optimism and hope!" Is this Christian hope?

A political candidate in another country promises that his program will bring justice and liberation to the poor; that this is inevitably true because the poor are the future of history, and history moves forward and cannot regress. Is this the Christian hope of the poor?

A friend tells the relatives of a seriously ill person: "Have hope, everything will turn out all right." Is this optimism hope?

An optimistic temperament is not hope, nor is a pessimistic temperament despair. Moreover, certain declarations of optimism usually cover over a deep despair.

Being sure of a better earthly future is not hope. The future is not in our hands, nor can we determine what it will be. Sometimes it is better, sometimes it is worse. Nothing in the laws of history assures us that history always progresses toward goodness and justice, or that it is irreversible. Experience confirms this changeable judgment.

Christian hope is not based on the laws of politics, history, or science, always fragile and ambiguous in their human application. Human freedom, always unpredictable, is capable of frustrating the most reasonable expectations and precautions. Hope is not the prospects or hypotheses of futurology. Hope is not the conviction that in human conflicts on whatever level the good always triumph over the bad, the poor over the powerful, the truth over falsehood. Sometimes yes, sometimes no. No one has ever said that life is always just, and that just retribution characterizes history. This is not pessimism or cynicism; it is human realism, freed of both pessimism and cynicism by Christian hope.

What, then, is hope? St. Paul writes: "In hope we were saved. But hope is not hope if its object is seen; how is it possible for one to hope for what he sees? And hoping for what we cannot see means awaiting it with patient endurance" (Rom. 8:24–25).

Christian hope is the security to obtain, possess, and enjoy "what we cannot see." If we saw it, with the senses, or with human logic, or with scientific or natural projections, then we would no longer hope. We would project into the future, with reasonable farsightedness, the consequences of present causes. To hope for progress in a country, or the end of a war, or a cure for cancer, is historical hope — also very important — but not theological hope, which is based not on the humanly foreseeable, but on faith, the content of which is unseen although it is certain.

Hope does not come from scientific or historical analyses, as trustworthy as these may be, but from faith. For this reason hope is inseparable from faith, and is of the same nature as faith. For "faith is confident assurance concerning what we hope for, and conviction about things we do not see" (Heb. 11:1). Faith is living and acting "as if . . . looking on the invisible God" (Heb. 11:27). Without faith there can be no hope, because what is hoped for has to be first accepted by faith.

What then properly belongs to hope? What distinguishes it from faith? *Hope is the firm conviction that the promises we know by faith will be fulfilled.* Not the whole content of faith is proper to hope, only the contents of the promises of faith.

By faith we accept that Jesus is God and that he reveals God to us. He reveals the mystery of God, the plan of God for humankind, salvation and the ways of salvation, the future of humankind. The revelation of God in Jesus Christ includes promises that are part of hope. These promises, fulfilled by the coming of Jesus Christ, appear already in the revelation of the Hebrew scriptures.

God promised to Abraham to "make of him a great nation" and that "all the communities of the earth shall find a blessing in him" (Gen. 12:2–3); "All the land that you see I will give to you and your descendants forever" (13:15). God promised, "I will make your descendants like the dust of the earth" (13:16).

To Moses God promised, "Now that I have heard the groaning of the Israelites, whom the Egyptians are treating as slaves, I am mindful of my covenant (made already with Moses' ancestors). I will deliver you from their slavery. I will bring you into the land which I swore to Abraham, Isaac, and Jacob" (Exod. 6:5–8). And through the prophets God centered these promises in the future Messiah savior, bearer of a universal reign of happiness and peace, of "new heavens and a new earth; the things of the past shall not be remembered or come to mind" (Isa. 65:17). Certainly the believers of the Old Testament already practiced and lived hope in these promises.

The promise of God begins to be fulfilled with the coming of Christ the Messiah. Christ is the promise, but he will not be the consummation of the promise except in eternal life. Christ is the promise; in him is the whole future reign of God, in hope. But hope is not the definitive consummation, but only the actual and certain, although obscure and fragile, experience of the promise.

The hope of the Old Testament was lived as a prophecy. In the new covenant, hope is lived as a present richness, which is the grace of Christ—always awaiting its consummation in glory. Therefore the revelation of Christ is about both the present and the future. This leaves room for hope; the present is enveloped in the night of faith, to become light in a future still unseen, but hoped for.

Jesus promised us that "he who feeds on my flesh and drinks my blood has life eternal, and I will raise him on the last day" (John 6:54). The eternal life of the children and friends of God already begins here, in a real way, although precariously and in limited fashion, and is given to us in communion with Christ. In its earthly condition this eternal life is vulnerable and can be lost. Because of this possibility of losing eternal life, its enjoyment forever is an object of hope. The full manifestation of this eternal life, in the resurrection, belongs to a future that passes through our own death. This future no one has seen, but it is hoped for, because of the promise of Christ accepted in faith. Hope is the certitude about what faith promises us.

In the Beatitudes (Luke 6:20–21; Matt. 5:3–10), Jesus promises the fullness and happiness of the Reign of heaven to the poor, the merciful, those who hunger and thirst after justice, the peacemakers, the pure of heart, and those persecuted for their goodness. The Beatitudes are one of the great promises of Christ and his new covenant. They are the promise as a lifestyle. Once again, this promise begins in the present. The poor and the merciful are already happy today and the reign of God has already begun in them. But the reign will only be manifested fully and forever in the future life. This is what we hope for. Christian hope is to live now already, in the invisible realm of faith, what we will see one day face to face.

HOPE AS THE FUTURE OF HUMANKIND

Hope looks fundamentally to the future of humankind in the light of the promise. God and the reign of God are the future of humankind, and hope is the experience of God and the reign of God as future.

The Bible calls this "the eternal reward," "the reward of the reign of heaven." Jesus himself encouraged the hope of his disciples with the future reward: "Your Father who sees in secret will repay you" (Matt. 6:4). The Apostles do the same repeatedly throughout the Christian scriptures: "Eye has not seen, ear has not heard, nor has it so much as dawned on man what God has prepared for those who love him" (1 Cor. 2:9). And in the Apocalypse, the book of the promise: "I will see to it that the victor eats from the tree of life" (2:7), and God "shall wipe every tear from their eyes, and there shall be no more death or mourning, crying out or pain, for the former world has passed away" (21:4).

The great mystics never hesitated to encourage the hope of their disciples with the idea of eternal reward, present in themselves. They had unquestionable reasons from the Christian tradition. First, the final goal of hope is eternal happiness, the inheritance and gift of the love of God, reward for faithfulness to our human and Christian vocation. Reward implies struggle, effort, and generosity to remain strong in hope. Secondly, the great trial and temptation of hope is the cross, failure, and suffering. To hope against all human hope is the stuff of a strong and mature hope. The reward due after the cross helped the martyrs and persecuted to hope against human hope. "I consider the sufferings of the present to be as nothing compared to the glory to be revealed to us" (Rom. 8:18).

Neither the scriptures nor the saints are timid or scrupulous in affirming the dimension of the "reward" of eternal life. Given their experience of human frailty and its need to be stimulated, especially in extreme situations, the saints did not think that a reward turned love into something mercenary. To eliminate the theme of heaven as a reward, as something belonging to "decadent religion," could be presumptuous and proud. Hope is not always motivated by love alone.

The radical object of Christian hope is the happiness of God shared as the future of humankind. But humankind has to participate in the construction of this future, contributing human freedom with love for the sake of the future. Therefore *Hope is also human commitment. Hope looks not only to the future but also to the present.* Hope is also historical and is nourished in daily life.

Hope is historical because of Christ, who already inaugurated for us the promise as the reign of heaven (his reign has already begun). We live already in the present life the richness and grace of this reign we hope for. The reign is like a growing seed. Heaven and eternal life have already begun in the heart of those who seek God and the good, through the action of the Holy Spirit, given to us as the pledge of hope. Because of the Spirit living within us, hope is not a desire for a future we have never experienced at all. Christian hope is the actual experience of all the good things we hope for as a permanent plenitude. This changes the meaning of life, our way of living, of dying, of acting, and the value we give to all things. Christian hope, like faith and charity, is incarnated in life.

HOPE AS CONFIDENCE

The incarnation of hope in daily life comes from the fact that the promises of God are anticipated in the present, as happens with all the dimensions of the reign of God. God is not only the future of humankind, but also the substance of its present. The saving love of God does not only welcome us into eternal life; this love is poured out each day over us, although veiled in faith, which leaves room for hope.

The projection of this hope in the present generates confidence in God. The theological tradition called it confidence in the providence of God: *God will provide us in the present with everything we need to reach the future promise.* This also forms part of the hopeful message of Jesus: "Do not worry about your livelihood. . . . The unbelievers are always running after these things. Your heavenly Father knows all that you need. Therefore seek first his kingship over you, his way of holiness, and all these things will be given to you besides" (Matt. 6:25–34).

This call to confidence in God is also part of Christian hope. The future promise is inseparable from the earthly path toward it. Hope is lived as a waiting for what has not yet arrived, and as confidence that God gives us every day everything necessary for the wait, in such a way that the wait is anticipated step by step. In the text quoted above, Jesus calls us to incarnate our hope by placing our lives in the hands of God with the same security with which we hope in the future. Therefore the wait and confidence are inseparable, and they either grow or decline together. For we have the right to trust in the providence of God, if we seek first God's "kingship over us and God's way of holiness." That is to say, if we live according to our vocation to eternal life.

Christian confidence is designed for hope. It is not an arbitrary or irresponsible confidence, one that would replace human effort.

We are obliged in any case "to seek God's kingship over us and God's way of holiness." Nor is it a confidence that hopes for anything whatsoever, or hopes for immediate fulfillment. We confide in God in virtue of God's promises, and these do not include everything that we humanly desire, nor what might seem necessary to us, nor are they realized according to a human time schedule.

For the promise on which our daily confidence is based is that humankind will be fully humanized and liberated in eternal life. The object of Christian confidence is that this promise will not be frustrated in the person who seeks the reign of God, and that in whatever social or human condition, God will give that person what is needed to continue to grow as a human being and as a child of God. This does not mean that all serious problems of life will be solved, that there will never be need or scarcity, that no apparently good project will ever fail, that incurable diseases or premature or incomprehensible deaths will never occur. For none of these are incompatible with the justice and holiness of the reign of God, with the friendship of God, with human fellowship, and with the happiness of each person.

God wills the happiness of everyone in this life, insofar as possible, and not that persons be merely "content." We continuously confuse "happiness" with "contentment." Happiness has a profoundly human, spiritual, and moral character concerned with interior fullness. Happiness is compatible with suffering, physical evil, scarcity, lack of satisfaction of certain earthly aspirations. "Contentment," on the other hand, comes from the pleasure and satisfaction of immediate temporal accomplishments, and for that very reason is of brief duration and incapable of filling life completely. Too many persons seek contentment and not happiness. Worse still, too many persons have no interest in true happiness, and prefer to live in the pursuit of deceptive contentment. The same thing happens with authentic happiness as with authentic freedom; too few persons want to be free. Because of this the Christian message touches on true freedom as much as on true happiness.

Confidence in God consists in believing that we will have the necessary means to resolve situations incompatible with the happiness of the reign of God and its growth in our midst. What situations are these? Often we do not know, just as we do not know what is and what is not suited to the growth of the reign of God in history. The promises of God do not deal primarily with temporal goods. The promises deal with human dignity and its growth toward eternity. In the history of each person we do not know what is the best relation between the temporal and the eternal. Health or sickness, well-being or poverty, success or failure? We do not know.

Therefore to place ourselves in the hands of God with confidence is an act of theological hope, which is inseparable from faith in a God rich in mercy. To place ourselves in the hands of God is also to have confidence that God knows better than we what is suitable for us, and that we will receive what we really need, not on our deceptive terms, but rather according to the wisdom of God. We will not receive what we need when we want, but when God wants, which is the liberating moment.

God's hour always arrives, for individuals, but also for societies. We do not know what is suitable for the happiness of societies, according to the justice values of the reign of God. What forms of social development are needed, and when? What political changes, and when? What type of material progress, and when? Because we do not have the answers to these questions, we cling to hope and historical confidence. For Christ is the Lord of history, and rules over it—on his terms, not ours—often in mysterious ways, so that "God makes all things work together for the good of those who love God" (Rom. 8:28).

Hope in the promise assures us of the definitive triumph of good over evil, of justice over injustice, of truth over falsehood, of love over hatred, of grace over sin. Hope assures us that the oppressed, the poor and suffering, are blessed because they will be liberated. But we do not know how the promise will be realized in terms of history. In extreme situations of dehumanization and evil, hope becomes radical—victory and liberation come with the death of the just one. But we do not see how the victory of good is anticipated in the history of each day. If we saw it, there would be no hope.

Like faith, this firm and mature hope is scarce. We can apply to hope the words of Jesus about faith, for both are inseparable. "When the Son of Man comes, will he find any faith on the earth?" (Luke 18:8). "If you had faith the size of a mustard seed, you could say to this sycamore, 'Be uprooted and transplanted into the sea,' and it would obey you" (Luke 17:6). It is a case of hoping at times against human projections, beyond the doubts, beyond what we see, in spite of the fears, the cynicism, the skepticism, and in spite of what at times is more difficult, the flattery and seduction.

2

Giving Reasons for Our Hope

"**S**hould any ask you the reason for this hope of yours, be ever ready to reply" (1 Pet. 3:15).

I have spoken of the nature and content of Christian hope. To do so is to give a reason for our hope: our faith in the Word of God sees in that Word a future promise. In God's self-revelation to humankind, God and God's promise are identical, and God and the future of humankind coincide.

In Christianity hope is an essential component of the very experience of God. We cannot relate to the Christian God without hoping and confiding in that God. Therefore as faith is an essential component of our experience of God ("Anyone who comes to God must believe that he exists, and that he rewards those who seek him"—Heb. 11:6), the same with charity ("Let us love one another because love is of God; everyone who loves is begotten of God and has knowledge of God . . . for God is love"—1 John 4:7–8). Hope is also an essential component of the experience of God ("We have come to know and to believe in the love God has for us"—1 John 4:16). For to believe in the love of God is to hope for what God has promised. The promise is the love of God manifested to us.

The ultimate reason for our hope is our conviction that God loves us, forever and without conditions, and that if we do not reject this love, we will have a future of indescribable happiness. The reason for our hope is the reason for our confidence in the love of God, manifested to us in a trinitarian form.

The very way the Trinity is revealed to us gives a reason for our hope. The Trinity is revealed to us as God the Father who has made us his children and prepared for us the marvels of the reign of God as our inheritance. That is the promise.

15

The Trinity is revealed to us in the Son, Jesus Christ, handed over for all of us to destroy the one impediment of the promise, the only source of despair, sin, and death. With Christ crucified and risen, the promise is irreversibly assured for us, and the way is open for us to achieve it. The ultimate reason for our hope is the risen Jesus.

The Trinity is revealed to us by the Holy Spirit, poured out into our hearts (Rom. 5:5), in the church and on the whole face of the earth, as a pledge of the hope that Jesus assured us of. The Holy Spirit is the anticipation of the promise. The Holy Spirit brings us to live hope as a spiritual experience. The Holy Spirit guides persons and events through the paths that lead to the promise. In each believing person and in the collective consciousness of the church and Christian communities, the Holy Spirit transforms apparently negative, disconcerting, and crucifying experiences into hope.

For the person who hopes, all is grace, all contributes to the realization of the promise because of Christ, the reason for our hope. But we do not see that all is grace (if so, it would not be hope), and at times we see the opposite. For this reason, Christ gave us his Spirit "who will guide us to all truth" (John 16:13), and will show us what is sin and justice (16:8), maintaining our hope in the mysterious ways of life.

The Holy Spirit is often impenetrable and surprising. We are not capable of deciphering the Spirit's personal and collective ways. Individuals, the church, history—they often seem to us to have been abandoned to their fate. A plan of love and a promise seem at times no longer there. But in the long run (in human terms) the Spirit never "loses" in the plan to advance the promise on earth and the growth of the reign of God among us, and especially in the plan to maintain the hope of our future. The Spirit is the finger of the Trinity; the Spirit points out the ways of hope in the labyrinths of our history.

In that history the great temptation and pitfall of hope is the persistence of sin, of evil, and of the suffering of the innocent.

HOPING IN THE MIDST OF THE EVIL OF THE WORLD

The mystery of evil is the great temptation against hope; it is also the proof of hope.

Faced with the God of the promise, evil seems to question the promise. Faced with the God of love, evil seems to deny love. From a human and historical viewpoint, evil is absurd. How explain the massacre of innocent persons, the persistent dominance of power and money, the everlasting oppression of the poor, the failure of the best and the apparent success of the worst, natural catastrophes that afflict the poorest of the poor?

For some, the absurdity of evil cancels out the existence of a personal God, or at least divine providence, and eviscerates any form of hope. The paradox, however, is that the evil of the world is one more confirmation of the existence and providence of a God of love, and is one of the reasons for hope. In life the "bad times," more than the good times, are times of hope, because hope increases as less is seen.

Christian hope is the difference between an absurd world without meaning and worthy of distrust, and a life full of meaning, worthy of confidence. It is the difference between life as absurd and life as mystery. Mystery is full of meaning. It is the projection of the promise over the absurdity of evil, revealing its underside of light.

How is this true?

First, a human being cannot possibly understand clearly the evil of the world. That would be like understanding God and God's universal designs, which is beyond human intelligence. It would be like understanding fully the mystery of life. To do that we would have to be like gods. It is not a question of clearly understanding life, but of detecting its mysterious meaning, a meaning reasonable and trustworthy—like God. This is possible through the faith filled with hope that God has put within us.

Secondly, the promise that is the foundation of Christian hope is not incompatible with temporal evil, only with eternal evil. Even more, the promise was necessary because of the existence of evil. It presupposes evil and suffering. The promise does not pretend to eliminate evil for us, but rather to give evil meaning in the light of a destiny of total good. "Affliction makes for endurance, and endurance for tested virtue, and tested virtue for hope. And this hope will not leave us disappointed" (Rom. 5:3–5). For in the last extreme, "fear him who can destroy both body and soul in Gehenna" (Matt. 10:28).

Thirdly, it is always useful to remember that the source of evil—of all moral evil (sin), physical evil (incurable disease), and natural evil (catastrophes)—is never God. God is the source only of good. God is incapable of generating evil as such. But why then does God permit it to exist, if God is all-powerful and could avoid it? Where is the providence that is part of our hope? The temptation posed by the problem of evil remains.

A few considerations illuminate this mystery. The key for approaching the mystery of God is not God's power but rather God's love. Certainly God is all powerful, but the guideline of God's providence and design for humankind is not the exercise of power, but rather merciful love. God is love (1 John 4:16) *and the use of power is governed by the use of God's love* for the world and for human beings. If God simply used divine power to suppress all evil, God would violate creation and especially humankind in its dignity and freedom. The mandate of love is to let others be what they are in their deepest identity. Permitting evil to exist is inherent to a God who transmits and respects life out of love.

In effect, it is essential for the world and humankind, which are not God but creatures, to be corruptible, to be able to fail, to have to end or die at some time. Moreover, for a human being to be human it is essential to be able to choose, to be able to opt for destinies and ways of life, to be able to make a mistake or act wrongly. The only way to avoid all this is not to create humankind or the things of this world. For example, from the moment that the sea exists, it is finite and imperfect, and tidal waves will occur. If the earth exists, it is perishable and subject to contingencies and faults, and earthquakes are inevitable. God does not order it that way. God allows it to be that way, because otherwise God would have to have made an absolutely perfect creation, which is contradictory in itself.

The same holds true for human beings. We are not God; we are limited in time and corruptible. We are destined to die; we can sin; we are subject to frustration. Sicknesses, accidents, suf-ferings—all are inherent conditions to our very being. The only way to prevent these evils would be not to create human beings. It is better to live human misery with hope than not to live at all.

For this reason God creates with love, even at the risk that human beings become corrupt and frustrated. But then, if the promise can be frustrated because of the human condition itself, and if evil and sin in all their forms are not only a risk but a permanent and consummated fact, where is hope? We are here at the crucial point of the problem of evil and its mystery. And the key to illuminate it is once again the love of God.

By the love that inspires God's power, only God can trans-form evil into final good, and make inevitable or deliberate evil work for good. The work of Jesus Christ makes this possible, and decisively so by his death on the cross. Jesus crucified is the ultimate reason for Christian hope, and the only possibility of overcoming the apparent absurdity of inevitable evil.

The apex of evil, the most absurd moment in the history of evil in the world, is the Son of God unjustly dead on the cross. The sufferings and the unjust crucifixion of Jesus are not paradigmatic; many much more dramatic deaths have taken place. What is paradigmatic of evil is that the crucified one is God. The torture of God is evil brought to its maximum expression of the absurd. God dead on the cross is an even greater mystery than the mystery of evil itself. Who can understand it? The evil of the world is incarnate in the crucified God. Because of the crucifixion of Jesus, we can give meaning to evil and recuperate hope. Why is this so?

The fullness of evil—the rejection and death of God—was assumed by Jesus with the maximum of love possible on earth ("God did not send his Son into the world to condemn the world, but that the world might be saved through him . . . for God so loved the world that he gave his only Son, that whoever believes in him may not die but may have eternal life"—John 3:17, 16). Because of the way Jesus assumed the evil concentrated in him, evil ceased to be incompatible with an attitude of love in the one who suffers it. Evil ceases to be absurd and becomes a mystery, which can be integrated—also mysteriously—with the mercy of God and God's loving providence.

The evil of God crucified, the symbol of all evil, can be the way to the ultimate good. This evil made possible the resurrection of Jesus to a full and eternal life. Because of the resurrection the evil we suffer, without ceasing to be evil, is transformed into the road to the promise. This is the reason for our hope in the midst of the evil of this world. The evil of the world, a massive and permanent fact due to the human and earthly condition, is reintegrated with the good we hope for because of Christ. The God of life, who had to allow evil to exist, redeemed it and liberated us from this desperate situation through an even greater evil (Christ on the cross). God was capable of avoiding the definitive triumph of the evil of the world and returning hope to us.

From now on, who can separate us from hope? "Trial, or distress, or persecution, or hunger, or nakedness, or danger, or the sword? As scripture says: 'For your sake we are being slain all the day long; we are looked upon as sheep to be slaughtered.' Yet in all this we are more than conquerors because of him who loved us" (Rom. 8:35–37).

In the extremes of evil, where its absurdity becomes even more incomprehensible than ever, in the abandoned of the earth, in those who face inevitable death, in the massacred and the tortured, in those trapped without escape, hope can be based only on its most radical foundation: Christ on the cross, about to rise and live forever.

HOPING IN THE RESURRECTION

Everything said so far can be condensed into one affirmation: the key to the problem of evil and the key that gives permanent validity to hope, is the resurrection of Christ prolonged in our own future resurrection.

In effect, the promise is not only guaranteed by the word of God. It is also guaranteed by facts, as befits the God of the Bible and of history. This God relates to humankind and communicates to humankind promises and saving grace not only by words, but also and equally by events. In biblical and human history, deeds and signs confirm the word of promise. These deeds and signs of promise, which appear already in the dawn of human history and multiply among the people of Israel, converge toward Christ. Therefore as Christ's word is the fullness of God's word, so Christ's deeds are the fullness of God's deeds, which reveal and guarantee the promise announced with words. The resurrection is the work, the act, of Christ, which sums up all his life's deeds of promise.

The resurrection of Jesus Christ is the unshakable guarantee of the promise. This Christian axiom points to the resurrection as the most specific and ultimate reason for our hope. It makes the resurrection the center of all the motives we have to believe and hope. St. Paul writes (1 Cor. 15:14): "if Christ has not been raised . . . your faith is empty too" (he could equally have written "your hope is empty"). And, he continues, "we are the most pitiable of men." This implies that for St. Paul the resurrection of Christ is the fundamental fact on which Christian faith and hope rest. It implies at the same time that faith and hope are unchallengeable and guaranteed, because in fact Christ did rise.

"Christ rose and lives forever as the eternal source of hope." This is the joyful announcement of the first Apostles, themselves witnesses to the risen Jesus. It is equally the substance of the Christian proclamation today: Jesus is alive; he is acting; he generates life and liberation; he is the radical cause of our hope.

The resurrection of Christ, witnessed to by the early church, gives the reason for our hope because it confirms the divine origin of the words and promises of Christ.

The resurrection gives the reason for our hope because with it the promised future life is really inaugurated. By rising as "new humanity," no longer subject either to evil or to death, Jesus creates a reality within the reach of every human being— a future of new life, absolutely renewed in spirit and in body, where death and all forms of evil are overcome forever. The risen Christ is for everyone hope itself, personified and incarnate, where all promises and hopes are concentrated.

The resurrection gives reason for our hope, because Jesus is not the only one to rise, but rather the first of all the risen. According to the explanation of St. Paul (1 Cor. 15:13–24), the resurrection of Christ will be followed by our own, and this is the quintessence of Christian hope: after we die we will rise like Jesus. For this reason our being should be open to an absolute future, and we should live in accordance with the life we hope for. "Since you have been raised up in company with Christ," St. Paul wrote, you should lead a new life. (Col. 3:14).

Yes, the resurrection of Christ is guaranteed by facts, but does our own resurrection have the same guarantee of significant facts? We have to answer this question decidedly in the affirmative. There is a human being, other than Christ, a creature like us, who has already followed the path of the resurrection after Jesus. She is the Virgin Mary, and her assumption into heaven is a fact that guarantees our own call to resurrection. Mary has already risen. She, the mother and the first follower of Jesus, was also the first to follow him into his future life. She, the first model in her faithfulness to the hope in the promise, is the first to participate in the fullness of hope. "Blest is she who trusted that the Lord's words to her would be fulfilled," her cousin Elizabeth said of her (Luke 1:45).

Marian devotion calls Mary "our hope." At first sight this might seem an exaggeration, for our hope and its origin is Christ. Nevertheless, Mary is in some way also our hope. As the first creature to accede to the fullness of the promise, she becomes for each of us one more reason to hope. For having already entered into the future life in body and spirit, Mary makes our hope more concrete, nearer, more human. The resurrection is not a theme of utopia or of religious science fiction. Through Christ we know that it belongs to the deeds of God in history, and through Mary we know that this deed, which for us is promise, has already become a reality for all humanity.

The resurrection gives the reason for our hope, finally, because in it the promise is fulfilled in an integral form. We will rise, like Mary, body and soul, and not only in spirit. The resurrection has a material aspect. It integrates spirit and matter. Therefore the promise of the future life is not only spiritual, but also material, integral. Not only new life, but also "new heavens and a new earth where . . . the justice of God will reside" (2 Pet. 3:13).

Therefore the risen Christ inaugurates a new world, a new justice, a new fellowship, a new reality totally humanized and renovated. The future life promised to humankind is not a life and a world of pure spirits, disincarnate, but rather a life that prolongs the corporal and material nature of humanity, although in a mode radically transformed and renovated. Risen humanity is not transformed into angelic life. It remains human, now fully so and incorruptible. Its condition of being incarnate, material, social, and collective, related to other human beings and to the world, continues, although in a different way, without time, without place, without limits, without decadence, sin, or death. We do not know the how of this new mode of being human after the resurrection, for we have no reference point in our actual experience to understand it. We are limited to time and place, to corruption, to evil and death, where matter does not serve the spirit, but rather often the opposite. But we do know that this new human life in new heavens and new earth is viable, because through Christ and his resurrection God has made us participate in a divine mode of being, sending us the Spirit who "renews all things," as an anticipation in history of this future life.

The resurrection of bodies signifies that in an absolutely new way history also rises. Human history—humanity with its aspirations, searchings, utopias, relationships of friendship and family—is totally purified and transformed, in the form of authentic happiness.

The resurrection is the link between hope in the future beyond death and hope that we must incarnate and try to realize in our values, already now in this world, by our efforts to do better. By reuniting in the resurrection body and spirit, future humanity with actual humanity (as the fruit is united with the seed), we are told that there is a relation of continuity between material creation and eternal salvation, between the hope we live today in faith and the cross, and its full realization in the reign of heaven.

The resurrection unites Christian hope with authentic human hopes in the one same project of God.

3

Eschatological Hope and Human Hopes

In our earthly condition Christian hope lives together with human hopes. Confidence in the promise lives together with the expectation of human liberations: a more just society, the overcoming of many diseases, the achievement of peace, or simply success in projects, family life, in the struggle for a cause.

Do these human aspirations or hopes have religious meaning for the believer? How are they related to the promise of future life, the foundation of eschatological hope? In fact, there is a profound relation in Christianity between this hope and earthly aspirations. But this relation is not simple, nor is it easy to realize in Christian practice.

There is a tension between eschatological hope and human aspirations. It is a tension proper to the nature of the reign of God and Christianity, incarnate and historical, and at the same time transcendent and future. This tension is due to the fact that both forms of hope—the purely human and the eschatological—are at the same time linked and separated in historical events as much as in human hearts. We should not separate the provident God of history, in solidarity with human misery, from the God of the future promise. Nor should we allow purely human aspirations to take the place of the promise in our hearts.

This is the temptation of secularism, which in some way or other is a permanent temptation to the human spirit: to put human achievements in the place of the promise. We need to develop this point.

THE MIRAGES OF HOPE

The temptation of secularism coincides with human history, and with the first announcement of the promise. It was the continuous temptation of the chosen people, Israel, and of the official religion of the Old Testament. This official religion rejected the prophets, who proclaimed authentic hope and denounced its substitutes. This official religion reduced the promise of the Messiah to a temporal liberator, the promise of the messianic reign to the future grandeur of Israel. It reduced the "promised land" to a purely geographic region and secular future wellbeing. It understood enemies of the people of God as their political enemies and historical oppressors. The values most proper to the messianic reign, which are the true content of hope, were reinterpreted in terms of the historical aspirations of a people.

In this context it was inevitable that the prophets be misunderstood or reinterpreted in a purely temporal way, and that later Jesus, inaugurating the messianic reign according to the authentic hope announced by the prophets, be rejected also. (See, for example, the parable of the tenant farmers—Matt. 21:33–45.)

The permanent misunderstanding with respect to Jesus, even by some of his followers, was this: Jesus announced the future of humanity and the promise of the Spirit, and this message of evangelical hope was reduced to the illusion of temporal aspirations. "I assure you, you are not looking for me because you have seen signs but because you have eaten your fill of the loaves. You should not be working for perishable food but for food that remains unto life eternal; food which the Son of Man will give you" (John 6:26–27).

This misunderstanding—the temptation to transform purely human hopes into a mirage of theological hope—continues after the time of Christ. This temptation comes with different messianisms according to the times and cultures, when Christians fail to integrate them fully with the Christian messianism of the new and lasting life. The unbelieving world substitutes earthly aspirations and messianisms for the Christian hope that it lacks.

The human being, oriented toward the Absolute, cannot live without some form of hope.

The substitutes (mirages) for Christian hope are usually of a religious or secular nature according to diverse cultures. *Religious mirages* include theocracies, more or less explicit; millenarian movements and expectations of the imminent coming of Christ in glory and of the proximate end of the world, which would realize the promise soon, in the present time. Another substitute for hope is the belief that wealth, material progress, and power are blessings from God and signs of election and salvation. This substitute is of Old Testament origin, but it is present in a hidden or open way in certain Christian confessions.

Secular substitutes for hope are predominant in modern cultures: the sciences and ideologies as "promises" of the absolute future of humankind. It should not be so. Science and the human progress it brings are an anticipation of the promise and should inspire us toward it. To realize authentic human hope is to search for the promise and to tend toward it with more force.

Scientific achievements become a substitute for the promise when humankind entrusts its present and future to them, when it places in them all its confidence, like the builders of the tower of Babel. But total confidence in what is seen or foreseen not only leaves no room for religious hope, but also condemns humankind to frustration. Science is not only limited in satisfying the human heart, it also cannot overcome the evil of the world—much less sin—nor give it an ultimate and hopeful meaning.

The same thing is true of the ideologies that attempt to create an always better future for human coexistence. These ideologies try to control the process of history and society. When an ideology is total, in itself or in the people who adopt it, it becomes existentially incompatible with religious hope. To think that human beings are capable of constructing societies and reaching historical stages in which there will be no moral evil or alienation leaves no room for the God of the promise, nor for Christ to realize the promise. Because ideologies are at least insufficient, if not ambiguous or partial, the earthly paradises that they offer lead persons from frustration to frustration. History teaches this lesson.

The substitutes of Christian hope, to the degree that they displace it, end in deception and desperation. In some cases, they degenerate into superstition.

THE SUPERSTITIONS OF HOPE

Superstition, with its many nuances, is a deviation of hope, a substitute for despair. Superstition is a permanent tendency of the human spirit, in all cultures and historical epochs. What changes are the terms and the areas of superstition. Its temptation persists, even in "advanced" societies, in ever new ways.

A superstition is something we believe in and which influences our lives. It has no scientific or religious foundation. In societies where religion is strong, superstitions usually refer to the religious dimension. In secularized societies superstitions have a more scientific or pseudo-religious reference. The widely held idea that superstitions are only deviations of religion is inexact. The world is plagued as much today by pseudo-religious or scientific superstitions as in other historical periods.

Religious superstition replaces hope with belief in promises that have no basis in faith: that this prayer or that devotion automatically "solves" a problem; that such and such a religious medal brings good luck; that placed on the door a medal protects the house from any material harm, and similar beliefs. Religious superstition is the abuse and corruption of hope, and distorts religious faith by placing it at the service of human aspirations.

In modern culture pseudo-religious superstitions replace hope with ungrounded promises: forms of spiritism, divining of the future, horoscopes that foretell the future, and the like. They are all answers, with no religious or scientific basis to the permanent desire of human beings to secure their future. Only the promise of God can do that.

Superstitions of scientific origin are more subtle but equally important substitutes for hope in the modern world. Psychology, technology, medicine, political science generate — not in scientists, but in many others — beliefs without a basis in reality. If we say that a little faith leads to superstitions, and that great faith is incompatible with superstitions, we can also say that a little science leads to superstitions and that great science is incompatible with them.

Therefore, for example, persons resort to psychological sciences with the vain hope that these can accomplish much more than they can in fact. Some look to them for interior happiness, peace, the elimination of suffering. What is really hoped for is the suppression of pain and the crosses that are part of the mystery of life. No science can do away with these. Each person has to learn to integrate them maturely with their life. Faced with the great questions of the spirit and of human relations, psychology is a limited substitute. In this field religious hope has no substitutes. The contrary would be a "psychological superstition."

In the same way, technology can create expectations of human progress and happiness that go beyond its possibilities. The world is full of false technological hopes — a qualitatively different life, the end of hunger and scarcity, and so forth — that constitute authentic superstitions and substitutes for hope. Especially common are those that come from medical science. Some persons hope for security in health and a control over the normal decline of the body through the years. Their hopes are superstitions and caricatures of true hope. Obsessions in some affluent cultures about health and what could harm it (beyond what is reasonable and scientifically proved) could be a symptom of the same thing.

There are also *superstitions of political ideologies*. These are inevitable to the degree that ideologies become totalitarian and offer economic, social, and political models to solve social evil, poverty, and war. Ideology attempts to substitute for God's promise and Christian hope. But ideology, in what it has of science, is incapable of substituting for hope, and it generates "political superstitions": pseudo-scientific affirmations that feed human expectations of a better future. Many of the real postulates of totalitarian ideologies require "acts of faith" and hope that correspond to a religion. Because of their lack of scientific basis they are nothing more than superstitious postulates.

For example, the ideological affirmation that collectivization of property makes human consciousness selfless and prone to solidarity, has no scientific corroboration. It is a form of superstition that requires an "act of faith" to be accepted. In the same way, the postulate that political systems in themselves lead to just and fraternal societies is a superstition that calls for a great deal of "faith," because historical sciences do not support it. That continuous production creates in time economic justice, that racism disappears with economic equality, and so forth, are so many forms of ideological superstition that require acts of faith that should be given only to the promises of God.

THE CHRISTIAN MEANING OF HUMAN HOPES

If on the one hand Christian hope has no substitutes, on the other it gives religious meaning to humanity's legitimate pursuits and authentic accomplishments of growth and liberation.

The Christian is identified first by adhesion to the promise of God, and by a way of being and acting proper to one who awaits eternal life, faithful to the road that leads to it. But the Christian's hope includes knowing the future promise is already inaugurated in the risen Christ, who works through his Spirit to anticipate in history "new heavens and a new earth" where everything will be better and more just (2 Pet: 3:13).

The Spirit's anticipation of the future promise is coherent with the same attitude of Jesus in his earthly life. He announced fundamentally the gospel of eternal salvation, but he accompanied his announcement of hope with his efforts to liberate persons from their human misery: sicknesses, evil spirits, hunger, social margination. By experiencing the fulfillment of their human aspirations these persons got a taste of eternal salvation.

Human hopes, in the perspective of the gospel, are signs that reveal and inspire Christian hope. They are like its "sacraments" on earth. By promoting good, justice, and peace, and liberation from misery, Christians are not only faithful to their own hope, but also help others to hope.

Nevertheless, human accomplishments should be measured in relation to the promises of God. They are not themselves the primary object of those promises, and for that reason they do not have a guaranteed fulfillment.

There is no promise that our human aspirations will be fulfilled. First, because we do not know which accomplishments are really humanizing, in themselves or in their consequences, or which ones are suitable for obtaining the promise, or which ones place us on the road to it. In classical terms, we do not know which earthly accomplishments are suitable for our salvation and which are not. With respect to salvation, we do not know what is better in concrete cases, sickness or health. God desires health and not sickness, but in a specific case, it could be that the evil of illness leads to a greater good that a person needs. Also, in concrete circumstances, given human frailty, poverty could be better than having money and a problematic life better than one with no problems. Human success is always in relation to the promise.

Secondly, the realization of legitimate human hopes, authentic human liberations, belongs to the responsibility and freedom of humankind. Persons frequently frustrate these hopes. The abuse of freedom, whose most negative form is sin, makes any human hope uncertain and insecure. Human hopes fail because of the evil that persons themselves perpetrate, frustrating their own aspirations. Humankind is incapable of overcoming or transforming evil and failure into good. Only Christian hope brings us beyond evil toward the greater good.

No frustration of earthly hopes should extinguish in believers their hope in God. Not only does the ultimate hope of humankind remain intact in any human contingency whatsoever, but also the values and fruit of hope can be lived and experienced in even the most negative conditions. In failure, in illness, in poverty, in oppression, the person of hope can maintain values that are the fruit of hope, values proper to the human vocation. Dignity, faith, solidarity, fellowship, a Christian atmosphere . . . all can be maintained.

Christian hope is the fundamental guarantee that human beings, in any system, in any condition, in any trial or apparently hopeless situation, can preserve integrity and dignity, can maintain their spirit free and with love, and can reach their destiny.

THE HOPE OF THE POOR

This guarantee of hope applies in a particular way to those who lack human expectations in the most radical form: the poor, those who suffer, the abandoned. Hope is offered to them as the great richness of their lives, at times the only richness. The poor and suffering are a radical "sacrament" of what we can hope for on earth against all human hope, a sign that the power of hope is capable of sustaining the values of the spirit even in oppression and on the cross.

The poor and suffering are the "preferential sacrament" of the humanizing and liberating value of Christian hope in the midst of human despair. This is one of the most important features of the gospel of Jesus. The poor are preferentially offered the gospel as a source of hope and profound happiness precisely because they lack human hopes. If "bad times" are a providential condition for growing in hope, then so are "bad conditions," for hope is offered with more force and clarity when its earthly anticipations are not experienced or seen. We hope for what we do not see (Rom. 8:24).

The strongest and most typical expression of the gospel's offer of hope to the poor was proclaimed by Jesus in the Beatitudes (Luke 6:20–23). By affirming that the reign of God belonged to "the poor, the hungry, and the suffering," Jesus offered them hope, in a privileged way, as a future of happiness and total liberation. No poverty or oppression of this world can take this away from them. But the poor and the suffering are also offered a taste of this definitive hope in the experience of their present lives, challenging the apparent despair of their human condition. This paradox converts the poor into privileged witnesses of hope.

The hope of the poor rests on an unseen dimension. Because of this fact, socio-political and economic provisions are important but insufficient in themselves.

The social sciences spell out the condition of the poor. They have no human hope of receiving the justice due them and the recognition of their dignity in society. The social sciences point out to us that poverty in the contemporary world has an ethical root. The mechanisms of economic systems impose poverty. These systems are dehumanizing. This is not the poverty of simplicity of life freely chosen, liberating, and humanizing in accord with the gospels. The poverty of the poor in today's world is an insult and a dehumanization.

The social sciences show us the complexity of the causes of socio-economic poverty and the difficulty in overcoming misery. This misery is rooted in social mechanisms of all sorts, in the economic interdependence of the world today. It is rooted in the lack of political will on the part of those responsible to make socio-economic changes in systems that create privileges of wealth or power at the price of the poverty and margination of the great majority of national populations.

The social sciences tell us that this inhuman poverty has increased in the last twenty years, and that given the political and economic realities of the international community today, there are no expectations that the poverty of the poorest regions of the planet can be overcome in the short or even medium term. The aspirations of the poor appear frustrated, at least for the present generation.

And, nevertheless, the poor have a right to hope. Not the poor of the future—those who will be alive at the time of the greatest justice and Christian liberation—but the poor of today; those who will probably die poor. The evangelical Beatitude is spoken of them. The richness of Christian hope is for each generation, whether it overcomes its poverty or not. Each poor person of today is called to be a privileged witness to hope, in the midst of apparent despair.

The poor are privileged witnesses to hope, because to the degree that they cling to hope, they can move already here on earth toward the happiness and dignity promised by God. The poor can conserve their dignity, in spite of every intention and circumstance to the contrary. The consciousness of their dignity is the root of their happiness (beatitude), here and now. This is not an empty theory; it corresponds to the facts. The experience of living among the poor and oppressed teaches us that there is a dignified way to ascertain that human misery exists. It is not always so, but it is a reality in all cultures and situations, particularly where there is a strong religious sense and a sound humanism.

We have all known persons who have lost everything and have not lost the joy of living; persons who are imprisoned unjustly and do not lose their peace and tranquility; persons who live in misery and take in orphans; persons who have suffered injustices and seek to reestablish justice with no desire for revenge; persons who in collective tragedies forget themselves and go to aid others. This and much more has no merely social or anthropological explanation. It is also due to the irruption of evangelical beatitude in the lives of the poor, which makes them witnesses to a radical hope.

The poor are happy (blessed) in their dignity, not with the "contentment" of the world, but with the experience of their friendship with God and with knowing that God loves them and that they are the privileged heirs of the reign of God. They are happy because of the experience that it is possible to maintain, in adverse conditions, a heart that is sane, kind, open, given to solidarity. They are happy because of the experience that their interior dignity, intact, is the motor of their aspirations and daily struggles for their human liberation, of which they never despair. The poor are privileged witnesses to hope because "they hope against all hope." They never cease to believe that they will be the protagonists of a more just and fraternal society, more worthy of the future reign of God, which hope promises and calls us to realize, beginning now.

In the poor we see hope in its most genuine and purified mode, in its most profound biblical roots. Hope is seen in the poor in the mode of Abraham, who believed against all hope (Rom. 4:18); in the mode of Job, who in sufferings and trials discovered and really experienced the hope of God, of whom he had only heard (Job 42:5); in the mode, finally, of Christ, the "Suffering Servant," anointed by the Spirit to bring to the poor, the captives, and the oppressed, the announcement of their hope (Luke 4:18).

In their seeking to be faithful to this announcement of hope, the poor—and in this case, all believers—have for a model and teacher a woman of their own condition: the Virgin Mary.

THE HOPE OF MARY

Above I referred to Mary as "our hope," for being the first creature to accede to the fullness of the promise. She is the first Christian, the first one to experience the total salvation of God: from moral evil through her immaculate conception, from death through her assumption into heaven. Mary is equally a model of the spirit of hope. She is the first Christian also because of the quality of her hopeful faith and for having been chosen by God to inspire and communicate hope to all. She is the educator of our hope.

From the beginning, Mary accepted the way of life that God showed her, a way often obscure and contradictory with respect to what the Lord had promised her—from the yes of a disconcerting annunciation through the yes of the helplessness of Bethlehem and the exile into Egypt to the passion and cross where the heart of Mary was pierced (Luke 2:35).

The hope of Mary will be the cause of her privileged sanctity and blessedness, and of her extraordinary mission to share her hope with the human race throughout all times, a mission that she already began in the beginning of Jesus' public life (see John 2:1–5, Mary's intervention in Cana). Elizabeth her cousin intuited the unusual quality of Mary's hope at the time of the visitation: "Blest is she who trusted that the Lord's words to her would be fulfilled" (Luke 1:45).

Inspired by these words, Mary responds with the Magnificat, the evangelical canticle of the Virgin. The Magnificat synthesizes and reveals the spirit of Marian hope, and the spirit of hope of all believers to come (Luke 1:46–55).

The canticle of Mary is the affirmation of a present, and of a prophecy. The Magnificat expresses the Marian hope in a God who saves now and forever (vv. 46–48), and her conviction that

God wants to extend this salvation to everyone (vv. 49–50). The divine promise is about universal salvation. She was the first to believe in it (v. 55).

The canticle of the Virgin expresses the Marian hope that this salvation be given as a total liberation from all human servitude, present and future. In God's future, humility will prevail over pride and the appetite for power; the poor and the hungry will be satisfied; the rich and the comfortable will remain empty (vv. 51–53). In the present, this promise is seen among the poor in their living hope, present grace, and human dignity. For if indeed it is true that the humble and poor will not prevail sociologically in every generation over the rich and powerful—nor is this a promise of God; and for this reason a predominantly social reading of the Magnificat would be incorrect—it is also true that the proud, the powerful, and the rich do not find in this life either the liberation from their servitude or their true happiness. On the other hand the humble and hungry do discover their dignity of being children of God, because they are the favored ones of the reign of God. They discover it in such a way that this dignity of the favored children of God leads them to maintain and continually struggle for the ideal of justice and fellowship. And in this ideal—at times realized during their lives, and at other times not—they find the values of the reign of God and the meaning of their lives.

Mary sang the Magnificat not only as an announcement of the hope her Son Jesus was bringing but also as the expression of her own hope as she experienced it at that moment. For Mary and through her for us, this hope consists of two things. First, that the God of mercy always fulfills the divine promises, from the time they made them to Abraham until the end of time. This is our hope. And secondly, that Christ turns human conditions upside down, so that arrogant wealth and power are not liberating, and humility and dignified poverty are liberating.

If Marian hope has a social significance, it is, surprisingly, that the ideal world is not a world with no poor, with everyone rich and satisfied, but the opposite. It is a world without excesses of wealth and power, where austerity and humanized poverty are the common way of life.

But this calls for great hope, the hope of the Virgin Mary, model and educator of our own hope.

4

The Education of Hope

Hope is life according to the fullness of a future poured forth by the Holy Spirit in our heart. This fullness is latent in us in the form of a seed, called to grow and develop until it fills life with meaning, integrating the unseen future into that life.

Hope is life according to the fullness of a future that is already anticipated in the experiences of daily life, even in things that are disconcerting and frustrating. Hope, like all values of Christian spirituality, participates in the incarnation. Hope comes exclusively from God, but it is revealed to us wrapped in human events. We do not possess it fully, since we hope for its future realization. But we can act, opt, and give a new meaning to daily living on the basis of hope. We do not see hope's promise, but by Christ's coming it is already being realized among us. We can discover its present realizations through faith and love, and thereby progressively educate our own hope.

Hope, always obscure and precarious, actualizes and reveals itself step by step in signs that manifest the triumph of grace over evil. These signs thereby nourish our hope. The word of God, the sacraments of the church, the testimony of the saints, all are privileged signs of hope. The gestures of self-denial and solidarity we see in others, the unity of families, the selfless defense of the weak and oppressed, gratuitous service given to human suffering, peace and equanimity in adversity, a capacity for reconciliation without arrogance — all are signs that hope has already begun to be realized among us.

Hope is educated by human experiences. Without them, hope does not develop. Our experiences vary: fullness, when we experience true love, friendship or fellowship; failure, when our plans are frustrated, or when persons we trusted disappoint us;

desperation, the product of extreme situations of moral enslavements, illness, or oppression without any apparent solution. For this reason the forms in which hope rises and grows also vary: the cross and fullness, desolation and consolation, were always complimentary and necessary ways to grow in any dimension of Christian spirituality.

The human experiences of *fullness* and *consolation* nourish hope when we recognize in them an anticipation—be it very limited and fleeting—of the promised happiness and wellbeing. *Crosses* and *desolation* nourish hope as purification and crises that lead to maturity. The painful void that they leave in human expectations rekindles the relevance of religious hope and gives the impulse to opt for this hope more freely and consciously. We see the value of light when we are apparently condemned to darkness; we appreciate the value of the future life when the present offers only desolation.

Hope grows through the warp and woof of our life, whatever road life takes—consolation or desolation ("all things work together for the good of those who love God"—Rom. 8:28). It grows with certain conditions and demands proper to a spirituality of hope. This spirituality does not grow automatically. Moreover, the experiences of life can often destroy hope. The realization of human aspirations, successes, and satisfactions often enslave us to the present, and blind us to true values and the necessity of future promises. On the other hand, the frustrations and failures of life can also lead to bitterness, despair, unbelief, and cynicism with respect to the consolation of religious hope. Successes and failures are two sides of the same temptation against hope.

What are the conditions for growing in hope through the living out of life? What attitudes are called for by the fact that every human experience can deepen Christian hope?

THE ASCETICISM OF HOPE

Hope is an essential part of the experience of God. The Christian mystics always reminded us that God is experienced here on earth not through the senses or by mere human satisfactions, but through faith, hope, and love, which reorient the depths of our being toward God. For this reason hope is a mystical experience, and as such requires an asceticism to develop. Asceticism eliminates the spiritual obstacles incompatible with faith, hope, and love.

Like all asceticism, the asceticism of hope consists in overcoming or purifying psychological habits, attitudes, and desires, to facilitate the living of hope. On this point the experience and teachings of spiritual masters like John of the Cross are very useful. When they discover the process of union with God through hope (a process that is part of the ascetical way of interior liberation), the spiritual masters emphasize the purification of memory and desire. Memory and desire are the psychological and spiritual supports of hope. Their orientation can either facilitate or repress hope.

Desire, a person's deepest attraction, is symbolized for the mystics by the "heart," in accord with the evangelical expression, "where your treasure is, there your heart is also" (Matt. 6:21). (The heart is the symbol of desire's love, which is the deep orientation of the will. The "treasure" is what the will desires. Its contents can coincide with the contents of hope, or consist solely of human aspirations. In this case the treasure is authentic only in appearance, and the heart is misled and divided.)

The spiritual masters help us to discern the content of our desire (the orientation of our heart), by looking to the passions that normally accompany it: joy, fear, and sorrow. These are not considered emotional attractions—we are not always masters of the spontaneous tendencies of our sensitivity—but as options that orient the will. In this case we can ask ourselves: What makes me joyful? What are my biggest fears? From what sufferings do I wish to escape?

For the spiritual masters, sincere answers to these questions reveal the desires and aspirations of the heart that give meaning to life. They reveal whether or not hope holds an important place in concrete life; whether or not our chief human desires are purified and reoriented according to authentic human values—those that correspond to our vocation and destiny—or only according to the immediate interests of "carnality." The Pauline description of Christian discipleship as living according to the Spirit and not according to the flesh (Rom. 8:5) applies adequately to the profound orientations of desire and its coherence with Christian hope.

How is the desire of the heart—and hope—purified and reoriented? For ethics as well as for Christian spirituality, a desire does not become an orientation of life until it is converted into an option of the will. The quality of our deepest options reveals the quality of our hope. Because of this *the reorientation and purification of desire* consist of the reorientation, or purification, or total change of our deepest options.

Reorientation and purification take place when we sacrifice a desire or an egoistical option in benefit of an option to serve God, others, and our true destiny. We reorient and purify desire when we sacrifice aspirations and "deceitful" hopes to opt (explicitly or implicitly) for the values of the reign of God and its promises. The sacrifice of the immediate leaves an ascetic emptiness in desire (the "nights" of St. John of the Cross). This emptiness is filled by the growth of hope, which inspires us to opt for what is still not fully seen. Each time we choose a better "treasure," our desire is purified and our hope grows.

In addition, the desire of the heart is reoriented and purified, and consequently hope is increased, when we educate ourselves to live the present moment with all the intensity and love we can muster, rooted in the promises of God. This is of prime importance for a spirituality of hope, and will require a special reflection later on. For now it is sufficient to remember that living the present in a Christian way is related to the purification of the memory. This is the second aspect of the asceticism of hope mentioned above, together with the asceticism of desire.

If faith requires the purification of the intellect (faith is supported by the intellect and reason, but goes beyond them), and if charity requires the purification of the will (one loves decisively with the will and not with the emotions), hope requires *the purification of the memory*. Hope orients the present life in view of the future, where the promised good lies. Hope, therefore, is living the present fully. In the present the future is constructed; in the present there is already participation in the future promises. Christian asceticism makes us take the necessary measures to resist the temptation to live in the past with its sterile memories, in order to be faithful to the present, inspired by the future.

Fidelity to the present presupposes a purification of the memory. Like every quality, the memory is a richness. But like every quality it can also build up or tear down, according to the use given to it. The memory builds when it conserves values, experiences, and recollections that humanize and enrich the present and thereby assure a future richer in experience. The memory makes us more thankful, more humble, because of past errors, more hopeful by recalling God's promises and what God has already done in us and others for the sake of those promises.

The memory paralyzes our present and weakens hope in the future when it keeps alive the deeds and experiences that have harmed us in the past. The memory paralyzes our present and weakens our hope even worse when it leads us to live the present conditioned by a sterile past, or simply to live in that past. To live in the past, to maintain the resentments and prejudices that paralyze charity, to cultivate failures, bitterness, and faults of yesteryear, are all attitudes of a memory incompatible with living the present with a heart liberated and disposed to build a future of hope each day. To purify the memory is to place the past at the service of that future.

This purification is not achieved from one day to the next. It presupposes learning to forget, and to learn to forget we have to love the only present we have, where we meet God, more than the past we no longer have. Like all aspects of the asceticism that changes hope, conversion of the memory leads us to live the present (see chapter 5).

THE CASE OF THE MAXIMUM SECURITY PRISON

Here is an example of the education of hope in conditions that would tend rather toward despair. The example is real, but not unique. In similar or different circumstances, we can discover it today in Christians everywhere, if we have eyes to see.

A while back, in Manila, in the Philippines, a nun friend of mine called to ask me to accompany her to a maximum security prison on the south side of the city. I had never been there, but I knew that a lot of political prisoners were there at that time. The occasion of the visit was the wedding anniversary of John, who had been in prison nine years. He and his wife, good Christians, are old friends of the nun, and wanted to celebrate their anniversary with a Mass in the prison. They invited me for this. The nun and John's wife would pick me up early in the morning and we would go together. I eagerly accepted, as an opportunity to practice the gospel ("I was in prison, and you came to visit me"), and also out of curiosity for a new experience.

John's wife picked me up in her car. They are a well-off family; John is a lawyer and journalist. She brought with her a basket of provisions, to lunch together after the Mass, and to give presents to some of the guards with whom they were friendly after so many visits. I could not find in her, or later in her prisoner husband, the slightest resentment or bitterness toward the personnel of the prison. The spirit of the visit was like a party among friends.

John was waiting for us at the entrance and brought us to the building where the things for the Mass had been prepared. During the walk there—which was long, since we had to go through most of the grounds—two things struck me. First, the human quality of the prisoners. They seemed relaxed, and every one of them greeted us amiably. Some came up to ask for a blessing, according to the custom of the Philippines. It was not at all difficult to strike up a conversation, even on the most personal level. Second, I was impressed by the religious atmosphere. The buildings were poor and completely run down, but as we went by they seemed more like a convent than a prison. The doors of the cells were covered with images of the Sacred Heart and the Virgin. These doors had no locks. The prisoners could enter and exit as they pleased, like a hotel. They moved around with no problem. I wondered about the "maximum security." Sayings from the Gospels were hung on the walls, like a retreat house, and in some places little altars were set up.

My new friend John told me about his experience in prison. He spent the first two years in solitary confinement. He tells the story in a matter of fact way. He took advantage of the time to write, read the Christian scriptures, learn to pray, review his life, and deepen his faith. Later he was very busy. He helped his fellow prisoners to write letters and judicial appeals. Many of them got their sentences reduced and are free today because of his help. Together with some others he started several prayer and Bible study groups. When he told me this I understood why many of the prisoners we met wore T-shirts with inscriptions such as "Prayer Group of the Holy Child." None of this has anything to do with the traditional image of a modern maximum security prison.

We arrived at the building where the Mass was to take place. Everything was ready. Some thirty persons had gathered, friends of John. Three of them had guitars and had prepared some hymns. The celebration, with such simple means, turned out to be very impressive. The participation was good, with several well-sung hymns in Tagalog. It was obvious that they went to Mass every Sunday. It was Lent, so we used the readings of the day, although in my brief homily—John translated into Tagalog—I did not refer to the gospel reading of the day. I talked about hope.

I really could not speak of anything else. Nor did I need to recur to a doctrinal treatise on hope or to my own experience, which at that moment I felt to be superficial and of little value. In the brief encounter I had had up to that moment with John, his wife, and friends, hope had acquired for me a new and tangible reality. Very seldom before had I been able to "hear, touch, and see" hope as I did at that moment. It had become terribly concrete. I had seen hope in the words, the attitudes, and the faces of these forgotten prisoners, living in dehumanizing conditions and, for the moment, without future expectations. As happens in extreme situations, in this case John and his friends found themselves faced with inevitable and radical options: desperation, emptiness, egotism, bitterness—or religious hope.

John had opted for hope, which God had offered him in the form of a cross, as Christ offered hope to the good thief. But to receive it John had to purify his memory and forget resentments and unjust experiences. He had to take his egotistical desires to find his own niche—human beings can get used to *anything* and find their niche in *any* circumstances—and reorient them toward serving others and communicating to them encouragement and hope. By living each day gratuitously, by serving others and forgetting any immediate personal interest, he could only cling to his values and to his ultimate future, lacking as he did at that moment any human promises. What he saw every day could lead another person to despair. For him it was a source of hope in what he did not see. The human and religious values of that prison could leave someone else completely indifferent. For him they were signs that future hope can be discovered and built in the present.

Toward the end of the Mass, at the moment of the communion, I had to break the hosts into small pieces. I had counted out twenty small pieces, but as the celebration progressed more people filled the place, and most of them wanted to receive communion.

Later, in John's cell, we shared the lunch among ourselves with his wife and the nun. With enthusiasm John told me of his future projects in the prison. Before going we exchanged addresses and he made me promise to call his daughters who live in New York.

We left the prison at the end of the morning, after saying goodbye to all those we met during the visit. As I left John, and during the whole trip across Manila from south to north, I had the impression that it was he who gave encouragement and hope in the farewells, and that for him his life in jail was just as full of meaning as if he were outside.

John's wife dropped me off at the parish. She was more affected by the visit than her husband was. I promised to visit them both when they were together again in their home. She told me that it would probably be soon. Before going into the rectory I stopped by the chapel to pray and reflect on the power of hope to conserve dignity and transform the meaning of any human situation.

THE FLOWERING OF HOPE

Hope can rise in any circumstances of life. Paradoxically, extreme and apparently hopeless circumstances create a void that calls more forcefully for hope. The case above is not unique.

The most impressive testimonies of hope are found in tragedies, wars, and irreparable failures. Hope seems to rise with the most force in the desert and desperation of life. How is this possible? It is possible if the heart is stronger than the adverse circumstances; if the heart has not emptied itself of dignity and love out of bitterness. It is possible when in human hearts there is room *for confidence in life, for selfless action, and for the risk of faith*.

Hope flourishes when it is practiced, when one acts as if its promises were real. Here, as in everything that concerns the human spirit, what is sown is harvested, and what is already lived is hoped for.

An attitude of *confidence in humankind and in life* is of prime importance. Without this basic confident outlook on life it is impossible to confide in the future promised by God, just as it is impossible to believe in the love of God without the experience of human love. Ultimate confidence requires confidence in the present. Hope is not "human" confidence, but to flourish it requires an attitude of basic self-confidence, confidence in others, and in the future. As a flower will not bloom without an appropriate climate, so also hope requires a context of confidence in life: life is not absurd; it has a positive meaning; humankind has a destiny beyond itself; evil does not have the last word in history; truth and justice will prevail; in every human being there is a spark of goodness and confidence. This is the human context, the "affective" context, that makes hope and its growth possible, even in (and often because of) greater adversity.

Maintaining life's dimension of gratitude, maintaining the *capacity to act gratuitously*, also make this hope possible. This is proper to all sound humanism, for persons become dehumanized if they do not understand or practice what is gratuitous, such as healthy friendship, service, art, or the forms of contemplation. Christian hope is facilitated by a healthy humanism, in this case, acting gratuitously.

Acting gratuitously means not seeking immediate gratification, not only in the material sense, but above all in the affective and spiritual sense (retribution, recognition, success, even interior satisfaction). This gratuitousness reactivates hope, for persons renounce immediate gratifications only for greater promises, according to the gospel parable of the banquet. This is a parable about hope in the gratuitousness of service to others: "Whenever you give a lunch or a dinner, do not invite your friends or brothers or relatives or wealthy neighbors. They might invite you in return and thus repay you. No, when you have a reception, invite beggars and the crippled, the lame and the blind. You should be pleased that they cannot repay you, for you will be repaid in the resurrection of the just" (Luke 14:12–14).

St. Matthew presupposes in the same way the spirit of hope when in his Sermon on the Mount he calls for gratuitousness in our actions with respect to God and others: "Be on guard against performing religious acts for people to see" (Matt. 6:1). In giving alms, do it in secret (6:3). "Whenever you pray, go to your room, close your door, and pray to your Father in private. Then your Father, who sees what no man sees, will repay you" (6:6). "Do not lay up for yourselves an earthly treasure . . . make it a practice instead to store up heavenly treasure" (6:19–20).

Hope depends on a promise that is not seen ("store up heavenly treasure") and does not look for immediate gratification ("lay up earthly treasure"). This is what we call *the risk of faith*: leave behind the vanity that is seen for the truth that is not seen. Hope becomes in practice the dimension of risk involved in believing in future rewards. If faith ran no risks, hope could not be tested, and if hope is not tested by the risk involved in gratuitous action, it neither matures nor grows. Every person of hope dies without having obtained "what had been promised,

but saw and saluted it from afar" (Heb. 11:13, referring to
Moses). And like Abraham—the paradigm of the risk of a faith
that generates hope—the person of hope in some way each day
"goes forth, not knowing where he is going . . . for he was looking
forward to the city with foundations, whose designer and maker
is God" (Heb. 11:8–10).

"Go forth . . . for he was looking forward to the city with foundations" is to run the risk of hope day by day. This happens
when one prefers service to comfort, the defense of truth and
justice to indifference, austerity to wealth, fidelity to duty to the
search for prestige. In the language of the Beatitudes (Matt.
5:3ff.), where Jesus gives a resumé of the spirituality of hope,
the risk is the option for mercy over judgment and the ways of
violence, the option for the experience of God over the vanities
of the heart, the option for the acceptance of the cross over the
deceit of egotism's satisfactions.

Nevertheless, human beings cannot live a style of hope so
radical that they need no experience whatsoever of the promise
already being realized in the present life. The spirit of hope,
because it is incarnate, looks not only to the future, but also to
the seeds of the future in the present. We call these *signs of
hope* in the world today. Part of the education of hope is to learn
to discover, discern, and contemplate them. They are the individual events and processes of liberation and humanization, of
reconciliation and solidarity: acts and gestures of fellowship, of
justice, of faithfulness to love, of forgetting self, of dignity and
peace in the face of crosses and adversity, of persistence in faith
in spite of hostility and persecution. In the sacramental order,
a sign of hope is the community celebrating the liturgy, announcing and accepting the word of God, participating in the eucharist, opening itself to evangelization.

All these signs can be seen with eyes of faith, and when seen
they generate more hope in the future, in the resurrection, and
in the promise. Or these signs can be seen as mere historical

and social events. In that case, the incapacity to perceive signs of hope and resurrection becomes in turn the incapacity to perceive and hope in God as the future of humankind.

For that reason the virtue of hope could not be experienced in fullness until it was inaugurated in present signs with the coming of Christ. Christ announced a lifestyle based on hope (summarized in the Beatitudes) only when the promise of the reign of God was being inaugurated among men and women by his coming. The Beatitudes are not only future promise, but also present experience anticipated as hope. The prayer that Jesus taught us is not only a petition for present successes and temporal wellbeing. The Our Father becomes in a special way the road to identification with God and to the desire that the promised reign of God come.

The spirituality of hope achieves the difficult synthesis that has eluded the human spirit in all ages. The human spirit is polarized between materialism and spiritualism, between the realization of paradise on earth and the cynicism and contempt for earthly achievements. This synthesis unites in the same hope the certitude of the triumph of good with the certitude that this triumph cannot possibly be realized in the present. It brings a realism with respect to the human condition, marked by evil and adversity. Hope is a synthesis between the patient waiting for a promised paradise and the unswerving effort to make a more human world. For in a more human world it is easier to recognize and live the anticipations of hope in the reign of God. "God promises the good of humankind, and the good of humankind is the vision of God" (St. Irenaeus).

Only in this synthesis is it possible to live any human situation whatsoever with dignity and hope, even those that would lead, without hope, to spiritual misery and desperation. The experience I had in the Manila prison is a witness to this fact. I am sure there are many other similar experiences. It is enough to look with eyes of the spirit to discover the impressive signs of dignity and hope offered by believers in Third World slums, or by believers discriminated against and oppressed in totalitarian countries, or by the victims of violence, hunger, and persecution who had to leave their homes "without knowing where they were going."

5

To Hope Is To Live the Present Moment

God promises eternal life for humankind. Eternal life is God, the ultimate source of all fullness. The promise and the hope it gives rise to is to live "like God" for all eternity.

Eternity is not time. It is not a time that will never end. It is a totality, a way of being for which we have no references in the created world. It escapes our present understanding, limited as it is to the imperfections of time and place. We know what eternal life is not, but we do not know what it is. If we want to explain eternity as God's way of living—an always insufficient explanation—we could say it is a permanent and infinitely vital "today." God is a "now" of total fullness, without past or future, as humans have. The Bible itself uses this image in different ways. (For example, 2 Pet. 3:8: "In the Lord's eyes, one day is as a thousand years and a thousand years are as a day.")

Through our hope—and in this case through our whole Christian spiritual experience—we begin to participate, already in our mortal life, in the life of God. Hope anticipates the promise of the eternal "now" of God. As a mystical experience hope relativizes the earthly past and future and emphasizes the present. For only in the present do we experience eternal life as the "now" of God that is God's own present. From this fact arises a tremendous paradox: the promise, which looks to the future, is assured only in our present; hope, which deals with future realities, can be lived only in the present.

The spirituality of hope, and everything that can be said about it—we reflected somewhat on it above—comes down to this fundamental affirmation: to live hope is to live the present, the "now" of our lives. What we called the asceticism of hope is related to the freedom and capacity to live the present, and what we called signs of hope are signified and signifying only for the

person who discovers them "now." This applies equally to all
Christian spirituality.

This spirituality characteristically pushes us to live the present as fully as possible; to take full advantage of this present; to
live this day as if it were our last ("as if we were going to die
as martyrs at the end of the day," says a spiritual writer); to
leave the past and the future in the hands of the God of mercy;
to be aware that only the "now" belongs to us, and so forth.
This characteristic of Christian spirituality comes from its dimension of hope, which inserts it into the "now" of God. It is
also possibly the most difficult demand of spirituality, going, as
it does, against all our tendencies and habits.

Persons dream, long for, recall, strive, and search for their
happiness in an uncertain future. The mystics, on the other
hand, who have learned to contemplate God in the present and
who have the wisdom to detach themselves from the past and
future (which does not impede them from repenting with seren-
ity nor from planning for the future with freedom), are among
those few persons who face with all their heart the requirements
of the present. At times these requirements are attractive; most
of the time they are not. At times we are called to relate to
interesting persons, but frequently this is not so. The present
can be very enriching; often it appears to be a waste of time.
But the mystic and the saint know that God is always found in
the "now" and only there. They know that we only experience
in each present moment the limited earthly happiness that God
offers us.

Many of the affirmations of Christian wisdom come from the
facts mentioned above. The affirmation that it is impossible to
relive true happiness from the past, or wait for it from the future,
but that we can find it only in the present; the affirmation, consequently, that happiness is rooted in one's self, in our inner
life, and not in external circumstances or events. For these have
their impact on us according to the total meaning we give to the

present, and according to the attitude that we have with respect to the past and the future.

From the fact that God is found only in the "now" comes the Christian affirmation that saving grace and love are continuously offered to each human being in their present, no matter how deficient their past; that we have to know how to recognize the "now" and take advantage of the grace that comes. For "now" is when we can prepare a better future, because the conversion, the light, and the discernment we leave for tomorrow never arrive. "Today, if you should hear his voice, harden not your hearts as at the revolt in the day of testing in the desert" (Heb. 3:7–8).

All this reaffirms the oft-repeated and somewhat paradoxical statement that Christian hope is not an "escapism" toward a heavenly future, but *the complete living of the earthly present.* Jesus himself continually insists on the same point, in terms of vigilance, of being alert now, of acting in each moment "in the light of day," and not clouded by our blindness and distractions from our past or the illusions of the future.

The vigilance that Jesus demands is the actualization of hope in each instance of life. We read in Matthew 24:37–44: when the Son of Man comes, "two men will be out in the field; one will be taken and one will be left. Two women will be grinding meal; one will be taken and one will be left. Stay awake, therefore! You cannot know the day your Lord is coming." This teaches us, first, that we should not trust that in some future moment we will be prepared to welcome God and our own happiness, for the Lord does not come in an insecure future, but in the present, which we can assure and prepare for. Secondly, it means what characterizes human dedication and fidelity to the present moment is not so much the tasks and circumstances of life ("be in the field...be grinding grain"), but rather the love and the hope placed in these tasks and the attitude with which these circumstances are assumed ("one will be taken and one will be left"). To be prepared for the "now" of God in our lives consists in having a living hope to receive God, and not in accomplishing extraordinary tasks on the margins of the ordinary will of God for our lives. Saints are persons who do not change their normal way of living, even knowing that that very day "they will be taken by God."

In the parable of the wise and foolish virgins, Jesus touches on the theme of how to prepare for his "now" with a hope always alive and disposed to welcome the Lord's visitation. All the virgins received the same call and the same opportunity to meet the bridegroom, only some had their lamps ready with oil (hope), and others did not. These latter ones were foolish because they fell asleep during the wait.

This leads to the other gospel theme that inspires us to live fully the present—the necessity to "be awake," and not to waste the present moment, which is a form of "being asleep." In Luke 21:34–36, we are warned (when the Son of Man comes, in the "now" of God): "Be on guard lest your spirits become bloated with indulgence and drunkenness and worldly cares (false hopes). The great day will suddenly close in on you like a trap. . . . So be on the watch." St. Paul echoes this same warning: "for you know the time in which we are living. It is now the hour for you to wake from sleep . . . the day draws near. Let us cast off deeds of darkness and put on the armor of light. Let us live honorably as in daylight" (Rom. 13:11–13).

For the Christian scriptures, "to awaken," "be awake," is to live "in daylight." Where does this light come from that allows us to live the present "as in daylight," that allows us to live the present as a full encounter with God and with our personal realization? It comes from a living hope. This way, illuminating the present—what the mystics call illuminating the darkness that blinds us to living fully—is the same as injecting hope into the sightlessness of our heart. For one of the forms of human blindness is the incapacity "to see" life as present, or to see the present as the source of happiness and fullness. The opposite of hope is spiritual blindness.

THE ILLUMINATION OF THE PRESENT

Psychologists also know that to help persons be happier, to relieve their anguish, depressions, or complexes, it is important to help them accept their present and live it as intensely as possible. Psychology offers different aids to that end. It helps persons to be more objective, to look without emotional blocks at the realities and circumstances in which they are involved, from the outside, objectively. This is liberating and brings people to see their present in a positive light. Psychology can also help us see ourselves objectively, from the outside, particularly in conflicts, in the face of attacks and criticism, in situations where we are emotionally involved.

Seeing ourselves objectively helps us to place in perspective what happens to us, to take away some of the drama, and to free us from fears and false interpretations. It helps us to identify the present as it really is, and ourselves as we really are, not as others would like us to be.

These and other psychological means that help us recuperate the joy of living the present are valuable aids for Christian spirituality. In fact, a good part of the mystics' orientations to asceticism—the asceticism that frees us for hope—is founded on a healthy psychological experience: *the liberation from our past*, with its accumulated prejudices that distort the present and our actual relationships with other persons. This liberation is from our past faults. These faults cast a shadow on the present not so much because of sorrow for having offended God, but because of our own pride when we become aware of our misery, when we become aware that our image is not perfect, and that the testimony that we give to ourselves is also not perfect.

The same liberation takes place with the orientations designed to *heal our relation with the future*—from anxiety, fears, and false expectations that ruin the present. The mystics tell us that desire and fear—always fear of not obtaining what we want or that something unfortunate may happen to us—are the two fundamental psychological attitudes in need of purification. They tell us that in both cases, at the bottom of it all, we have a false concept of happiness. Here spirituality goes further than psychology, since it alone can give us the true meaning of human happiness. Spirituality tells us that *happiness in inside us and is enjoyed in the present*. Spirituality tells us that the fear of losing happiness and the desire to acquire it are illusory, since the good or bad events of the future give or take away happiness not by themselves, but by the interior attitude with which we assume them.

Spirituality also goes beyond psychology when it affirms that the most secure and stable way to be objective about our reality and ourselves (to see ourselves from the outside) is through an attitude of humility. For humility is the truth with respect to one's self, and in the measure that we grow in it we make ourselves invulnerable to criticism, to the image we project, and to the judgments about us that others make. Humility is refusing to overvalue self; it is the forgetting of self. Humility is the conviction that we are not so important—in spite of perhaps holding down positions considered important; the conviction that others' opinions—or in this case our own opinion of ourselves—change nothing of what we really are.

Like hope, to which it is always joined, *humility is also an illumination*. The attitude of humility is not only acquired by the psychological experience of failure or other such experiences but also by the light that God bestows on us in our "now." This light was also promised to us. By it we see ourselves in our naked truth, and we see especially that everything is God's grace, and that if we forget ourselves and our "importance," we discover this grace in each present moment. We discover that this is what really counts, this is true reality, and not the vanities that enslave us to the past or to future illusions.

But humility would be useless if it did not open the way for *the illumination of love.* Christian love is the fruit of faith and hope, and is inseparable from them. Love is our response to the gratuitous gifts of the promise we already enjoy "now."

For this reason the mystics teach us that the quality of the way we live the present is measured by the love we put into each instant. Inserting love into each instant is not to feel love, but to always practice good and bring that good to others. It is to know that we are loved by God at every moment. It is to place the future in God's hands, forgetting the past. The mystics add that "if we put in love, we will take out love," and that "we harvest what we sow." With this the mystics mean that if we try, still filled with blindness and misery, to put love in each moment, we will have the light to experience the love that God offers us in that moment. After all, to hope consists in living the present. Paraphrasing a great mystic, we can say that in the evening of our life we will be judged by this hope.

THE DESIRE FOR GOD

We can draw the following conclusion: more than an intellectual conviction, to live the present is an existential experience. This experience grows according to the love we are capable of instilling into each moment. But if love is not a sentiment but a practice, how can we verify that that love, and the hope that goes with it, is present in our hearts? The mystics answer us that the presence of love corresponds to the intensity of our desire for God.

The desire for God is the positive side of the purification of desire. As an existential experience it includes two aspects that Jesus himself pointed out in the Beatitudes: "Blest are they who hunger and thirst for holiness (an intense desire for God); they shall have their fill." The first aspect is an intense desire to love; in Christian mysticism to desire to love is already to begin to love. The second aspect is that this desire can be "satisfied," now and in every moment. This aspect is real experience, because the desire for God is inseparable from hope, which assures us that to desire God is to already make God present in us. To desire God in each moment is to anticipate possessing God in the future life.

But the desire for God in the present moment is never fully satisfied. On the contrary, it tends to increase to the degree that we experience it. For the desire to love goes together with the fact, which we experience also in every moment, of our lack of response to the love that God offers us "now." We are always debtors with respect to God's love and God's promises, and our consciousness of the "debt of love" grows when our desire increases—as the fire grows when we throw on more wood.

In the mystics the experience of not responding adequately to God's love is dominant. It explains their other experiences of fidelity to the desire for God: the conviction of their own vanity and of the little value of their works, qualities, accomplishments, and apostolates, in comparison with their permanent debt of love. They confirmed this debt in each moment. It explains their asceticism for the purification of the past and of their future desires, in view of living fully the present. All their purifying asceticism, in the last term, is to strengthen, and in no way substitute for, the presence of the desire for God. Therefore the mystics' criterion for deciding what to renounce is the relationship to desire. In practice it is not a question of renouncing or purifying all that interests us or that we desire with our sensitivity, but of renouncing *what takes away or weakens our desire for God*. From this comes the spiritual saying: "Renounce nothing; but stay with the desire for God alone."

For the desire for God is God, just as hope is already living the content of the promise that is God. For this reason God is found "now" to the degree that God is desired with all the force of our spirit. ("You shall love the Lord your God with your whole heart, with your whole soul, with all your mind"—Matt.

22:37.) This strong desire for God is not necessarily incompatible with other desires of the senses, which are at times legitimate, and at other times not (they are temptations), with the condition that they are not transformed into substitutes for the only desire that comes from hope.

To avoid substituting sense desires for the desire for God, *the desire for God must be efficacious*, and not only a mere feeling or a wish. The desire for God becomes efficacious when it leads us to imitate Christ in his same desires, in his attitudes and practices of love. This imitation is never perfect; it is always insufficient. The experience of mediocrity and its candid recognition sustain and augment the desire and the efficacious search for improvement.

Lastly, the mystics warn us that this desire for God has to always have a dimension of waiting and a dimension of *personal love of God*. The loving desire for God is "direct" in Christian mysticism. That is to say, the practice of this desire is not realized purely by "serving God in others," or doing our duty according to the will of God (all of which is necessary in Christian practice), but rather that the desire for God presupposes always seeking intimacy, friendship, and the personal presence of God in each moment. For God and the love God offers cannot be reduced to or dissolved in any creature (not even our neighbor); God is desired and loved as God.

The desire for God as God is coherent with Christian hope. With hope we expect Christ to liberate us for the future and give us the means to reach that future. We hope especially for God as our fullness and happiness. For the promise, after all, is God, just as the desire to live it in the present moment is the experience of the personal and immediate love that God has for us.

6

Hope and the Transformation of the World

One of the most legitimate aspirations of humankind is to transform the world for its own fulfillment. This is the human task. Work is central to humankind's self-understanding, central to all humanism, at least in the West. Work is also central to Christian spirituality. By transforming created realities, the human being imitates God as creator of the world and generator of life in all its forms, to make the world more habitable and happier. We know from the Bible that God destined humankind to be lord of the earth and that God entrusted to it that same earth to be humanized (Gen. 1:26; 2:19).

Because of this commission to humanize creation, human beings have almost an innate confidence in the results of their work and a confidence in their action to transform the world, create cultures, progress scientifically, and reform societies. At least in the Judeo-Christian tradition, this confidence in human action is clearly perceptible, precisely because of the biblical doctrines of the creation and the mission given by the Creator to humankind—the image and likeness of God in this as well—to transform the earth.

This *confidence in action* is equally an element of the spirituality of hope. Confidence in action, precisely because it is integrated into the horizon of hope, eminently eschatological, has nothing to do with the ideology of action and success, so notorious in certain contemporary cultures. Nor does it consist in having many great ambitions and aspirations. It consists in being always open to the future, in the sense of being confident always in a better future—because of the promise—even though this better future is seen to be indefinitely postponed. To be open to the future is to have confidence that human action is not in vain, and that even failure has a meaning as experience, as a corrective, as redemption by the cross. To confide in action is to have a positive outlook on the world, confident that human beings can transform it for the better.

This Christian outlook, confident about the possibilities and future of the world, participates in some way in the contemplative attitude of faith and hope. For the future of humankind and the world is not based on an ideological confidence in human capabilities and science and technology. These are extraordinary on the one hand, but on the other they are insufficient — and at times counterproductive — to humanize and sanctify the world. This future is based on the largess of the creator God and on the seeds of goodness that inhere in creation. To discover these seeds requires faith, hope, and a contemplative attitude. It is often necessary to "believe" in the presence of a good God, creator and provident, in the midst of the tragedies of society and history, and of fatalism vis-à-vis the cosmic world.

For this reason the believer has an outlook of *basic confidence in the world*. We are speaking as much about the material world, the cosmos, as about the world of cultures and societies, creations of humankind. The attitude that one has about the world depends on the ultimate meaning given to it. Belief and unbelief, theology and materialism, find here their lines of division.

If the world is not a creation of God, or has no permanent relation to God; if the world has no goal, no ultimate meaning beyond matter or itself; if the world is not in the first place the dwelling of humankind and the place of human growth, then the world remains essentially unpredictable and blind — in spite of human action to dominate it — and can terminate in the absurd or in nothing. But if God is the origin and the future of the world as the place where life is transmitted; if the world exists to be humanized, and humankind is for God; and if the world in some way has also been rescued and liberated by Christ from meaninglessness and the absurd (Eph. 1:10; Col. 1:15–20; John 1:3–4, etc.), then the created world also has to be, in some way, integrated in the ultimate horizon of Christian hope.

A MATERIAL WORLD WITH HOPE?

According to the Christian scriptures the world "awaits" in a certain way the redemption of Christ. St. Paul writes (Rom. 8: 19–22): "The whole created world eagerly awaits the revelation of the children of God. Creation was made subject to futility, not of its own accord but by him who once subjected it; yet not without hope, because the world itself will be freed from its slavery to corruption and share in the glorious freedom of the children of God. Yes, we know that all creation groans and is in agony even until now."

This difficult text suggests several things. First, that creation, "made good" in the plan of God (Gen. 1) and in harmonious relationship with humankind, was also harmed in that relationship because of original sin and aggravated by social sins and abuses of nature. Evil is also present in the world; not a total domination of evil, but a disintegration and lack of equilibrium, like human beings after they sin. ("Creation was made subject to futility, not of its own accord but by him who once subjected it.")

Secondly, a quiet hope exists in nature of one day overcoming this damage and imbalance, and of recuperating its harmony with human beings (the humanization of the world). ("The whole created world eagerly awaits . . . yet not without hope, because the world itself will be freed from its slavery to corruption . . . all creation groans and is in agony even until now.")

Thirdly, this redemption that creation waits for is related to the redemption of the human race by Christ. The liberation and recapitulation of all things in Christ has humankind as its first and privileged object. But through humankind this liberation touches the whole human condition and the created world — society, history (Christ is the lord of history), and the cosmos (Christ is the lord of creation) (1 Cor. 15:27–28; Rev. 21:22; Col.

1:15–20). ("The whole created world eagerly awaits the revelation of God . . . to share in the glorious freedom of the children of God.")

History and the cosmos are only contaminated by evil, not completely dominated. The human condition, society, and the course of history are contaminated by social sins: injustice, violations of dignity and of human life, violence, hatred, idolatries of power, wealth, pleasure. . . . The cosmic world is contaminated in its harmonious relation with humankind. The cosmos is at times a threat to humankind (natural tragedies); at other times the action of humankind to transform the world is perverted and becomes a threat to nature. The whole question of ecology, of the preservation of the environment, of plant and animal life, and even the search for quality of life, has to do with the responsibility of humankind to humanize its relationship with the natural world, to transform it without demolishing it.

After sin, the human task of transforming the world takes on a new dimension. The task is now not only to dominate the world, to develop and advance it, but also at the same time to humanize the world, purify our relationship with it, empathize and be in harmony with it. We are not only called to better ourselves, anticipating by our sanctification the promise hoped for, but we are also *called to better "our world," advancing thereby our promised humanization*. Because of this all action and human work is called to be something sacred in itself, sanctifying for humankind, and humanizing for the world.

Human beings can really change the world, inspired by their hope in the promise of "new heavens and a new earth" (2 Pet. 3:13). This makes believers confide in the future. It makes them confident of the value of their actions and work, when these are directed to better the human condition and the world.

Human actions to transform and better the world are carried out in three dimensions: evangelizing, making personal relations and situations more human, and progressing materially by dominating nature.

Evangelization is the most excellent form of humankind's action on the world. It is aimed directly at the human spirit, not only to humanize, but especially to sanctify it. The sanctification of humankind is the root and the source of all the other forms of the humanization of the world, because the dehumanization, evil, and sin of the world have their ultimate origin in the perversion of human hearts. Evangelization frees hearts from their perversion and reveals true humanism and the ways to attain it. It especially reveals that "the person is more than a human being." The person is the subject of God's promises of a new life for all eternity, experienced already through the grace of Christ. The action of evangelization sanctifies humanity, making it participate in the life and experience of God.

For this reason evangelization, as human action, paradoxically goes beyond human possibilities. Humankind can humanize, but cannot sanctify. Only God sanctifies directly, through means instituted in Christ and contained in the church. Because of this, evangelization is a unique human action; it is realized in the church and convoked by the church. Its results do not depend so much on our efficacious action, but on the action of Christ—the prime evangelizer and sanctifier—who is with his church until the end of time (Matt. 28:20).

Because of this, finally, evangelization is the most trustworthy and certain form of human action. It is, therefore, the human action that deserves the fullness of our hope. To evangelize is to practice hope, because, differently from other secular actions of humankind (e.g. productivity and artistic creation), its fruits are not immediately perceived. Sanctification and preparation for the future life are, in the final analysis, in the hands of God.

The second dimension of human action on the world is the *humanization of personal relations* in society and cultures. They too are contaminated by sin and need to be healed and liberated. To humanize these realities means, on the one hand, uprooting from them whatever they have that is destructive of human dignity and of the vocation to live in friendship with God and in fraternal relations with others. On the other hand, it is to reorient the history of humankind according to the law of love and shared life. Therefore social, political, cultural, educational, and familial actions transform the human condition according to God's promises about the future of humankind.

The third dimension of human action is the *transformation of the cosmic world*. This is the role of the natural sciences, technology, and material progress in general. Ideally, this action has the objective of humanizing the natural world. This involves making the earth more and more habitable for all, where nature and matter are ever more at the service of human growth, eternal happiness, and ultimate destiny.

For the believer, action on the cosmos is also a form of healing it of the evil that contaminates it. This puts creation in harmony with humankind and the lordship of Christ. Needless to say, this would not be possible if science and technology were not subject to the service of humankind's future according to Christ. Therefore science and technology must be subject to the law of love and to the law of the primacy of ethics over blind progress. The imprint of God is present also in the cosmos, and this imprint has to be respected. The manipulation of material creation has a limit; to go beyond it with a false concept of progress makes the world less habitable and humankind less human in the long run.

If we place the world within the global project of the lordship of Christ and within the horizon of Christian hope, the question arises for the believer *whether or not the cosmos has a place in the future life*. Although to my way of thinking it is not made explicit in the sources of Christian revelation, nor does it form part of the faith of the church, it appears theologically sound to affirm that just as our bodies and human relationships will form part of the future life—although totally transfigured by the resurrection as a "new creature"—so also cosmic nature will form part of the future life, although equally transfigured and as a "new creation" (2 Pet. 3:8–13).

Through the incarnation, the man Jesus assumed the material world as part of his human condition, for it is proper to all peoples to be situated in the cosmos and be related to it. Theology teaches us that what Christ assumed, he also redeemed. From this it follows that the redemption and lordship of Christ is extended to all of creation, human as well as cosmic. This lordship, on the other hand, is exercised in the form of the redemption, healing and sanctification of everything created, including the cosmos.

Moreover, the future life that awaits humanity after the resurrection leaves persons as human beings and does not transform them into angels or pure spirits, even if it does imply the glorification of humankind. The resurrection transfigures, spiritualizes and fulfills, but it leaves intact the corporal condition of the human being. In the same way then, it would appear that the material and sense world should form part of the fullness of humankind in heaven, and contribute, in some way, to its eternal happiness—although in conditions absolutely different from those of the actual cosmos, and with a mode of materiality that we cannot imagine.

The words of St. Paul to the Romans (8:19–22), commented on above, suggest a future liberation for all of creation. What would this full liberation of the cosmos and its decontamination from every form of "sin of the world" consist of? In what way would matter contribute to the glory of God and to the eternal happiness of humankind? We do not know. But we do know that it is a question of other matter, of another sense world, and, for us, of another body and another sensitivity, radically transfigured.

7

Death, the Supreme Act of Hope

Death is the most dramatic experience of human existence, even for the person who lives in hope. It is an experience that cannot be repeated or communicated to another person. It takes us out of the human community forever, destroying the present moment and every earthly aspiration. We die absolutely alone and stripped. Only the crucified Christ accompanies us.

Our attitude toward death thus becomes the touchstone of our Christian faith. Faith is not proved so much by conviction about the existence of God—this is not exclusive to Christianity—but by the conviction that God is resurrection and life eternal for us. For this same reason death is also the touchstone of Christian hope; in death we choose definitively the promise over the despair of nothingness.

Death for this reason lends itself to temptation. For many persons it is the last temptation against their hope. As much as hope may have been tempted throughout a life—by the failures of the most cherished ideals and projects, by all sorts of frustrations, by the apparent uselessness of the struggles for and dedication to a cause—nothing is comparable to the temptation that death produces in some persons, as the absolute and irrevocable frustration.

But the paradox lies in the fact that, for God, the hour of temptation is also the hour of grace, and the radical temptation of death brings the grace of a radical hope. This explains why, against every human consideration, a human being can die in peace, a peace that in the midst of the agony of death can only come from God and be the last fruit of the spirit of hope.

If the spirit of hope is capable of changing the meaning of life, it also changes the meaning of death. Death concentrates the hope we practiced in life. Death concentrates our poor attempts to imitate Christ in the supreme imitation of dying as he died. If we can die with hope, it is because Jesus taught us to do so. This apprenticeship, part of our Christian life, is not realized overnight. It is realized during life to the degree that we learn to hope. To learn to hope in the promise is to learn to die according to the promise.

Learning to live and learning to die are inseparable. Even when we seldom think of our own death, we are learning to die by our way of living. Fear of dying and fear of living usually go together. Death is always welcome and without fear for holy persons, because they were not afraid to live faithful to hope. Paradoxically, death gives to a life filled with hope its ultimate meaning. Without death we cannot satisfy the most radical hope of a human being—to live forever. *Death decisively frees our love* and our search for happiness. The gap between what we are and what we would like to be, between reality and our aspiration for happiness and plenitude without boundaries, is bridged in death. This is impossible in our earthly life. Through death we can pay our "debt of love" to God.

In sum, in death the promise is fulfilled "for me." In death, finally, our precarious present, our "now," during which we tried to be faithful without much success, begins to participate in the present of God. Our "now" becomes eternal. Our desire for God, nourished by hope and always ambiguous and incoherent, is satisfied for ever. For with death all the servitude that obscured this desire is broken. Through death we define ourselves forever in favor of love. In death every form of egotism and corruption of love dies. In death only the desire to love remains alive. Only the love we could muster during our life survives, and that is the only thing that accompanies us.

In death hope ends. Fulfilled love remains. For we hoped for what is not seen, and when we die we see "face to face" what we were hoping for. We understand thus the affirmation of the saints: for hope to be transformed into love at the end of our lives, it is necessary to have lived faithful to hope when it was not evident, and faithful to love even when it did not fulfill us.

Therefore the way of asceticism and the purification of hope arrive at their culmination in death. *Death is the last purification of the person.* It is the most radical and efficacious purification, because of the agony and suffering it produces, because of the nakedness it brings us to, because of the patience that goes with the wait for God. Death purifies the memory of the past. This past can no longer paralyze us; it can no longer continue deceiving us or burdening us with its guilt, because it has already been dissolved in the mercy of God.

Death radically purifies our expectations and desires about the future. We can no longer expect anything from the future. Our human hopes, valid or deceptive, have been irreparably destroyed. In the moment of death the future is nothing—except the promise and the suffering face of Christ, which announces the promise as imminent.

We cannot accomplish fully, alone and with our own strength, this purifying transformation that the experience of death gives us. We need *the company of the church*, which in the name of Christ teaches us to die just as it teaches us to live. From the cradle the church makes Christ present to us as the teacher of hope, and helps us to follow him in our life, even in his way of dying. Paradoxically, the church, whose message for us aims at our living the present with fidelity, has been preparing us for death throughout the itinerary of our life. This action of the church, teacher of life and death in the name of Christ, is most revealing when we participate in its sacraments.

The sacraments, apart from all that the faith of the church teaches us about them, have a particular significance for hope. *The sacraments are signs of hope.*

In effect, the sacraments are an encounter with Christ in the history of our lives. This encounter is real and communicates life, just as the disciples of Jesus in the Gospels put themselves in contact with him and received from him salvific life. Unlike the Gospels, however, since Jesus is no longer physically present among us, it is not a physical encounter, but sacramental; the grace of Christ is offered to us wrapped in human signs, such as bread and wine.

In this context, participating in the sacraments revives our hope; it revives the desire for God and the will to satisfy this desire forever. It revives the desire to encounter Christ no longer through the partially obscure mediation of the sacraments, but in the fullness of the "face to face." This is especially true in the eucharist, when the encounter with the living Christ, and the hope that this gives rise to, reach their maximum intensity. In the very words of Jesus, to celebrate his eucharist and commune with his body carry the promise that the sacramental encounter will be fully personal when he returns to be with us (Luke 22:14–18; 1 Cor. 11:26). The transition between the two moments takes place at the moment of death.

For this reason, using mystical language, death is a "sacrament" for the person who believes, hopes, and loves. With death the relevance of the sensible signs ends. In death we meet Christ face to face, without the sacramental "wrapping." The sacraments of the church have already fulfilled their function of sanctifying and educating hope. From now on the Son of God will be himself our life and our light (Rev. 22:5).

What should we think in the meantime of the "death" of so many human projects, both personal and collective, that have failed forever? What should we think of so many frustrated efforts and struggles in service of others, at the service of peace, justice, fellowship—frustrations that are so many forms of "death"?

In truth, history does not resurrect nor can the past be re-created. Failures are often irreversible facts, at least for the persons, societies, and generations that experience them. They die before seeing the fruits of their efforts. We can certainly say that the experience, the ideals, and the mystique needed to take up again failed projects usually arise from the defeats and failures themselves. There are ideologies that affirm that "every battle lost assures the final victory of the war." A "mystique of failure" really exists; the idea that unjust deaths assure future justice and that holocausts are the guarantee of a better world. But is this true? What is it founded on? The experience of personal and collective history teaches us that there are many good causes that are lost forever and many good actions are never recognized. The irreversibility of many historical failures is one of the ways in which the sin of the world expresses itself. The recourse to optimism or to purely human hopes is useless in many cases.

Does Christian hope have anything to offer to the "deaths" of projects and failed good works? If Christ is lord of history and of human societies, these, certainly, are also an object of the promise. This is so fundamentally because the final triumph of good, justice, fellowship, and peace are assured in the "new heavens and the new earth" of the future life. But is this sufficient to give hope "now" to so many good works apparently lost and to so much generosity given to a frustrated good cause?

Therefore, the same as for personal death, Christian hope offers the fact—equally mysterious but real—of the solidarity of all humanity in the good that the faith of the church calls "the communion of saints." *Solidarity in the good* is not merely a law of history or sociology—of always limited application—by which persons of different generations and places would take advantage of the accomplishments, inventions, and examples of others. Solidarity in the good through the communion of saints is a "law" of the saving grace of the risen Christ. For this reason solidarity is also promise.

The communion of saints, the solidarity of all humanity in good, is universal solidarity in salvation. Our good acts of service to a cause, of struggle for the good (both on the personal and collective level), even those acts lost and failed in the eyes of the historical sciences, are not lost in the saving plan of Christ. They remain integrated with this saving plan. They benefit others. They have a repercussion as grace for others, in persons, times, and places that only God knows about. Efficiency and success are not the only things important for salvation and the construction of the reign of God among humankind. What counts is the love given. Love, faith, and hope are all values that cannot be accounted for by the laws of history, but they can enrich and influence the context of salvation and grace.

The great conviction of Christian hope is that *love is never lost*. It continues beyond our death, beyond failure, transformed into grace and salvation for others, because of the solidarity of all humans in the mystery of Christ, the unique source of grace and salvation.

The church—the place where we encounter this source and where we experience in a privileged way this mystery of communion in the grace of Christ—also educates us throughout our lives in the universal solidarity of spiritual goods. It induces us to pray for the living and the dead, and for every form of need and human misery. It inspires us to offer our lives, what we do, and what we suffer, for the growth of the reign of God among peoples, societies, and human enterprises.

Truly the church is the witness that Jesus left among us to introduce us to hope.

8

The Church,
Witness to Hope

The hope of believers, and of all those who look for a trustworthy motive for hope, has to be proclaimed, for itself and because of its source, by a sure, public, and universal word. In the same way, hope has to be nourished in its very roots. If not, it withers and dies, like a plant without water. Christian hope has to be witnessed to in a tangible and public manner. Otherwise it would be falsified by substitutes and would-be imitations, with no counterbalance. For if despair is a collective evil, nourished by the shadows and frustrations of human society until it enslaves the heart of humankind, hope also must have a collective witness.

That collective witness is the church. This is the church's *raison d'être* as organized, symbolized, and communitarian Christianity. On the one hand, the church is the assembly of all the communities, dispersed throughout the world, which unite all those who live in Christian hope. The church is the people of the God of the promise.

On the other hand, the church serves by keeping alive the hope of the world. For that purpose its community is endowed with the Bible, with the living tradition of the Apostles incarnate in persons, with the liturgy and sacraments that signify and communicate hope. The church preaches the God of the promise. Our faith and confidence in the church as a collective sign of hope among nations, and the certitude to fill the human heart with hope until the end of time, is a necessary part of the Christian experience and of the spirituality of hope.

The church proclaims hope. This is the essence of its preaching, from its highest magisterium to the evangelization by Christians in the heart of the masses. Perhaps now, more than ever, the Christian message should accentuate hope, its content of new life beyond death through the resurrection, and the anticipation of that new life in the present through signs of God's merciful love. The Christian message should assume human reality, arising above it and then returning to it, in order to see that reality with the eyes of faith. But the message cannot remain in worldly reality, satisfied with analyzing it according to Christian ethics.

This reality has to be illuminated by the light of hope. We have to see foreshadowings of eternal life in the signs of life offered by reality. We have to perceive in the signs of death a call to purify hope. For in the view of hopeful faith, evil and human miseries are not permitted by God as a punishment — the God of the promise does not send arbitrary punishments — but are permitted as a way of purification and as an invitation to a new life. In this sense all reality leads to the good of those who search for God.

Preaching that does not refer to the fullness of hope runs the risk of concentrating on denunciation of the world's and society's evils and miseries, leading its hearers to discouragement, conformism, or despair. Human realities always lend themselves to this. That was the attitude of the disciples of Emmaus when they evaluated the reality they had lived during the days of the passion. Their depression was the fruit of forgetting that God's promise was still in force and had been so in the previous days. They were lacking the recourse of hope. Jesus appeared to accompany them, to reeducate their hope, to remind them of the promises of God in the scriptures. The disciples knew of these promises, but not well enough to use them to illuminate a disappointing reality. Christ in Emmaus is a symbol of the church that evangelizes a problematic reality with hope.

In the world we know, many persons seem to have no reason for repentance. They appear to think they have committed no errors, past or present. That blindness places the unrepentant beyond the reach of the promise to be reborn to a new life. They lose the horizon of hope. The novelty of the evangelical experience lived in the sacramentality of the church is that the recognition of faults and errors ceases to be a purely psychological fact, ambiguous and capable of creating guilt complexes. These faults and errors become an experience of the hope that liberates from evil, from guilt, and from complexes. By calling us to conversion and to penance, the church does nothing other than convoke us to the new life promised by hope. The strong desire that persons feel so frequently to "begin anew" if possible, to "leave behind" the faults and errors of the past, in many cases to "live like a different person," can be really achieved by transforming utopian desire into hope by virtue of the sacrament of pardon.

But above all, as we well know, hope is most nourished by the sacrament of the eucharist. The eucharist commemorates the paschal mystery in the history of the world and in the center of the reality of our lives. The pascal mystery is the new and definitive life of the risen Christ, the reason for our hope. Because of the promise, Christ's suffering and death brought him to the resurrection, which overcame forever evil and death.

In the same way, in virtue of the same promise, the eucharist, which incorporates us as church into the pascal mystery of Christ, assumes our human reality and grafts it on to the life of the risen Christ. Therefore, with the hope of a promise whose effects have already begun, we can overcome evil in everyday life and death in the future. When we receive the body of Christ, we receive the seeds of the resurrection, and we can begin to live as "risen." We can live with a lifestyle shaped by the values of hope.

The church is thus the witness of hope in the flesh of its members. Hope becomes a significant message, not only when it is preached and communicated in its substance, but also when it is lived by persons. The Christian scriptures call the witness of hope sanctity, and the witnesses saints. The church reminds us that sanctity is the vocation of all Christians, and effectively, all Christians have something of the saint to the degree they live in a way consequent with hope. All Christians are witnesses to hope to the degree they are saints. They are "the light of the world," "the salt of the earth," "the yeast" (Matt. 5: 13–16; 13:33), according to the quality of their hope.

But there are different degrees. The witness that makes the church project itself as light among the nations is not constituted only by the accumulation of ordinary witnesses, but more by those who have lived hope to an eminent degree. These are the saints par excellence. Their belief in the promises of God freed them to achieve a heroic degree of love in the ordinary things of life.

It is very important that there be saints proclaimed as such by the church. They are identified with the hope that the church proclaims. They nourish our poor hope. The saints, fragile and vulnerable beings like us, inspire us to live faithful to the still unseen promises in joy and in sorrow, in success and in failure, in darkness and in light.

Mary, of course, occupies a special place. She is at the highest point of sanctity. She incarnates the hope of the Church. From the "yes" of the annunciation at the dawn of Christianity, she was the first to hope in spite of seeming contradictions, opening with her hope the way for the coming of Christ. Afterward her hopeful faith would not only be personal, but also maternal. Jesus would associate her with his work, and after that with the birth of the church, and forever with the church's growth as the people of God, pilgrim of hope. The hope of Mary intertwines with that of the church, and that of the church with hers. Both collaborate with Christ in the maternity of our hope; both are masters and educators of the way of our hope.

THE HUMAN DIMENSION OF THE CHURCH: TEMPTATION FOR HOPE?

The evil of the world is a temptation for hope. Many add to the evil of the world another source of temptation: evil in the church. Its historical deficiencies, weaknesses, countersigns, the sins and scandals of its members, would make the church a stumbling block in the way of hope for some, instead of what it is called to be—a source of hope.

The affirmation that the church is a stumbling block is not very rational, even though it has an undeniable existential and emotional force. It is not very logical—the logical and normal thing is that there be evil in the church—but it can serve as an excuse for some to leave the church. What is at stake here is something deeper, the human dimension, the humanity of the church. For it is clear that if the church is human—not God but a creation of God—it is composed not only of the Spirit of God, but also of persons, not only spiritual and invisible, but also a historical reality, it has to share the human condition: that includes limitations, errors, and human misery. To want a church without deficiencies and evil is the same as not wanting a church at all.

On a deep level the stumbling block for many with respect to the church, even for believers, is its humanity. Many actually seem to want a superhuman church, even though Christ, when he constituted the church, chose another way, the only one possible. He wanted a church totally human and totally inhabited by his Spirit of truth and holiness. Only in that way would Jesus save the identity of the church as a continuation of himself; Christ was totally human and totally divine, in the same person.

Going deeper still, the crucial point of the church as a temptation refers, in the last term, to *the humanity of Jesus* and to Christ himself as a temptation: "Blest is the person who finds no stumbling block in me" (Luke 7:23). There is a parallelism between the human condition of Christ and the human condition of the Church, with the only difference that in Christ there was no sin. This difference, as important as it is, does not resolve the problem that occupies us. I shall return to this shortly.

The humanity of Christ is a great mystery. God needed this humanity to enter fully into our history to liberate us. It was needed so that our friendship with God could take on a human face, so that our human destiny and ideal could have a model to follow. The humanity of Jesus was necessary so that the inaccessible God could become accessible to us. The man Jesus leaves behind him for all times the sacrament of our encounter with God.

The Christian paradox is that the humanity of Christ also and inevitably obscures his divinity. If God becomes man, this man participates unavoidably in the situation of the created, with all the limitations proper to the human condition. These limitations obscured the glory of God in Christ. For this very reason access to this glory always required, and still requires, faith. Access to glory is not evident. Because of this, many who walked with Jesus in his time did not believe in his divinity. His humanity gave them a pretext not to do so. The same thing happens today in a similar fashion.

In the humanity of Jesus there was no evil or sin. On the contrary, his humanity incarnated love and holiness. It was the perfect model of the impossible ideal of the church we form for ourselves — that it be the unequivocal witness to sanctity. Nevertheless, and this is the heart of the problem, the absolute holiness of Jesus was not enough for him to avoid being a stumbling block for many. Jesus, the Holy One of God, was disputed, debated, rejected by many, and misinterpreted by others. Then, as now, it was impossible without faith to recognize God in that man.

The humanity of the Son of God was, for those who were prepared in their heart, a sure way to meet the divinity. The words and works of this man were enough. But for those who were not prepared, the humanity of Jesus offered pretexts for not accepting his divine mission.

But let us return to the church. *Its human and historical condition is inevitable.* It must be a church formed and directed by human beings if it is to continue the work of Christ. From this fact we have to presuppose that there will be evil in the church. But even if the church were humanly perfect, like Jesus, it would still be exposed to criticism and would be for some a source of temptation. It is a mistake to think that a church with members absolutely faithful to the gospel would make the Christian message necessarily credible. It did not happen that way with Jesus Christ; "no slave is greater than his master; no messenger outranks the one who sent him" (John 13:16). Because of its earthly condition the church is submitted to contingent circumstances, to the culture and options of its leaders, to making some decisions that necessarily exclude other decisions probably equally as good. This exposes the church to criticism and doubt, even if what it does and decides is always morally good.

In fact the church is indeed criticized and doubted. The church is not usually accused of actually doing evil or of betraying the gospel, but it is accused of inadequate pastoral options, inopportune disciplinary measures, or of being conservative, leftist, anachronistic, or utopian. It is accused of many other things, according to the circumstances of the moment and the place in which it makes decisions and expresses its teachings, and according to the expectations and perceptions of those who give their opinion. That is the price of a church that speaks to and is submerged in human contingency.

Popes, bishops, and others have to appoint delegates and make decisions that always admit of legitimate alternatives, just as any community that lives on the earth and not in heaven. No matter how much wisdom and prayer support these decisions, they cannot avoid the criticism that comes from alternative and equally contingent viewpoints. Faith that the Holy Spirit assists the church, which leads believers to accept it even in its contingency, does not do away with human perceptions that limit its historical action.

To wish for a church of always optimal and incontrovertible decisions is to wish for an inhuman church. Or for an inhuman Christ. Or for an inhuman God, who does not take persons into account. It is to place the values of hope beyond our reach, for we have access to hope from that which apparently contradicts it. (We hope for "what is not seen"—Rom. 8:25.)

Therefore, like the humanity of Jesus, the human dimension in the church, paradoxically, is *one more reason to increase our hope*. This can happen when the heart is prepared to discover the anticipated life of God, not apart from, but enveloped in the human. The human frailness of the church and its representatives, always joined with its capacity to transmit life, roots us in the hope for a God who acts in us in spite of the limitations of the church. For hope is about the unseen, not the seen. This Pauline expression applies to the church, which transmits hope to the world in spite of its own fragility and in spite of such patent human evil.

As bearer of hope, the church is a symbol and a mirror of each one of its Christians. We also carry hope in vessels of clay; we carry the frailty and evil of the present and the already anticipated glory of the future. Christians see themselves in the church and place their trust in it, just as the disciples saw themselves in Jesus, identified with his humanity, and put all their faith in the divinity resident in him.

In sum, *our hope is the hope of the church*. Like faith, we receive it and nourish it by communing with the church. From the church we learn not to falter in hope. For in spite of the

misery that permeates the church because of its human condition, it has never ceased to announce and celebrate, with a persistence that can come only from the Holy Spirit, the true hope
of humankind and history.

9

Hope as Charism: The Religious Life

Ever since Christian hope has been in existence, because of the resurrection of Christ, what we call today religious life has existed in the church. Even before the church oriented and gave it norms, even before any institutionalization, even before anyone arrived at the synthesis we have today, the values, fragmentary at the beginning, of contemporary religious life were lived by Christians guided by the intuitions of the gospel. Placing goods in common, promoting fellowship, practicing detachment and austerity, choosing virginity for religious motives—values that today are integrated in the very identity of religious life—were all chosen as forms of life by many disciples of the Risen One. The Christian scriptures, as well as early Christian literature, give proof of it.

We could say religious life began to take identifiable and collective form with the desert fathers and mothers as early as the fourth century. Their *lifestyle* is inspired by a hope that seeks to be as consistent as possible and uses radical means so the "seductions of the world" do not weaken it. Their flight to the desert to search for the promises of God alone were a gesture of breaking with everything that could substitute for or distract from that search. Their radical way of living the baptismal demands did not yet become a form of consecration taken up by the church, but it led them to live the letter and the spirit of the three traditional vows. Their life of renunciation created a vacuum of human aspirations. This was necessary so that their human needs might be filled to overflowing by the spiritual experience of the future promises.

With time these first experiences of "religious life" evolved toward *the fraternal life in common*, as the normal context of consecration to God, which the church would establish as a necessary element of religious identity. (The juridical and public form of religious consecration had and has many variations, but its spirit is invariable.) By orienting religious life toward the fraternal community, the church understood that this community forms part of the public witness to the values of the future life. The religious community makes no sense without the shared hope in the promise of God to reunite all persons in love after the resurrection.

Religious life, which had begun with a variety of personal vocations, often partial in their content, but coherent in their evangelical reference, was *institutionalized by the church*. That assured its fidelity and development. This happens with every charism that should last through time without losing its identity. Synthesizing and simplifying, we could say that throughout early Christianity, religious life accentuated its lifestyle as a witness to the future life. With the passage of time, and more clearly in the second millennium and in modern times, the religious life began to emphasize *mission* and *the apostolate*.

Announcing and communicating hope was perceived more and more as coherent with the witness of a life founded purely on hope. Being and acting motivated by great hope are the two dimensions of religious life; they need and mutually reinforce one another. Some congregations will emphasize mission as total availability; others will emphasize the witness of life. But in some way or other all of them have to achieve a synthesis between living hope and bringing this hope to the lives of others.

THE CHARISM

Contemporary theology affirms that religious life is a charism, because it forms an eschatological project and lifestyle; *its present renunciations throw into relief the future* in Christian life. For no one can renounce present values in a healthy and free way if superior future values have not provided them with an experience capable of filling their life. This is precisely what is proper to hope. Religious life is a charism oriented to witnessing to the eschatological dimensions of life. Religious life is a charismatic way of living out hope.

What constitutes the charismatic in the way that religious life lives out hope is not, however, the mere fact of renunciation. For renunciation is part of all Christian life. It is a condition to remain free from everything—persons, things, circumstances—incompatible with the values of hope. "None of you can be my disciple if he does not renounce all his possessions" (Luke 14:33).

Proper to the religious charism (its radicalism) is that it not only renounces what is incompatible with the values of hope—sins, defects, attachments, lack of freedom, and the like, which is simply part of being Christian and being human—but it also renounces authentic human values compatible with the values of hope (marriage, the right to create a financial institution, or an autonomous activity . . .). These renunciations, for being unusual or radical, give witness to the relativity of human values in relation to the absolute values of the future by the fact that they are freely undertaken. The church and the world need this form of testimony, which inspires them to remember wherein lies the true treasure of the human heart (Luke 12:34).

Moreover, and this is equally proper to the radicalism of the religious charism, these renunciations of "good things" are made as a *commitment for life*. They constitute for the religious his or her permanent style and profession in life. (This consecration to God is usually called "religious profession.") From this we can affirm that the commitment "forever," with which the church identifies religious life (which does not take away the eventuality that the church itself can issue dispensation), is connatural to it. For every human being renounces occasionally something good and legitimate, to opt for better values. But what is proper and peculiar in the consecrated life is that these renunciations are not occasional but permanent, as part of a style and life project.

We have to add, lastly, that this style and life project is not realized in a private way, but in the church, *as community*. Community is an element proper to religious life. First, because it is a collective witness of the church, it has more force and value than a personal witness. Moreover a witness rooted in an ecclesial community has more guarantee of authenticity and continuity than an individual initiative. Secondly, because the religious community is in itself a product of hope, it bears witness to hope. For what is proper to a religious community—and this is also a charism—is that its members want to live in communion, in spite of all their human limitations, not motivated by temporal initiatives, flesh and blood, mutual advantages or interests, or any other of the motives for which persons form community, but motivated essentially by faith, hope, and charity. And this says to the rest of the church and to the world that charity is a reality among men and women because of faith and love, and a reality stronger still than flesh and blood or any other purely temporal motive. This witness also says that what hope promises—"new heavens and a new earth," where justice and love reign forever (Isa. 65:17–18; 2 Pet. 3:13)—is so true that it can begin to be realized here on earth, although in a precarious and fragile manner.

Up to this point I have emphasized how religious life witnesses to Christian hope by its lifestyle. I have to add to this an emphasis on *mission*. In this aspect as well, religious life is equally charismatic, radical, and a witness to hope. In addition, mission cannot be separated from consecration to a form of life; religious men and women consecrate themselves also to mission (according to their own charism) and make mission a prolongation of their consecration through vows. Mission, in the same way, is constitutive of community. It is another ecclesial element that unites. Mission belongs to the community and is realized in its name.

CONSECRATION AND MISSION

The radicalism of the communitarian testimony of religious life can be condensed into two points: consecration and mission.

Religious consecration, which the church synthesizes in the three vows (chastity, poverty, and obedience), radicalizes lifestyle according to the gospel. The existential value of the vows is that they renounce, by a special call from the God of the promise, legitimate values that for most persons give meaning to their lives and constitute the horizon of their aspirations and desires. Pleasure, possession, and power in themselves are not evil, and if they are lived according to gospel morality, they form part of a healthy humanism. But at the same time they constitute the most common sources of temptation against hope and the area where the idols and the substitutes for hope most easily arise.

Not every form of pleasure is renounced by consecrated celibacy, only a very significant area. This should be sufficient to generate in the person consecrated to celibacy a spirituality and a lifestyle of freedom with respect to all pleasure. Not every form of possession is renounced by poverty, only its most significant forms. This should generate in the person who has renounced possession an attitude and form of life detached and free from the need to have. Not every form of power over one's own life and that of others is renounced by obedience, only a very profound area of the exercise of will. This symbolizes and generates a spiritual attitude of searching for and submitting to the will of God in everything and above all else.

The spirituality of consecration by the three vows is a spirituality of freedom to welcome most fully, already in the present life, the values of the promise of God.

But religious life is not a project of life that has meaning only in hope. Because of that fact, religious also have to consecrate themselves to proclaim to others the hope that gives meaning to their life. That is mission. *Consecration to the missions* of the church is an integral part of the charism and radicalism of the religious vocation. The mode and circumstances of this mission are variable, from the missioners who leave their country to evangelize non-Christian peoples and cultures, to the contemplatives who offer their lives in silence that the world be converted to hope. This corresponds to the variety of charisms in religious life, but all charisms tend to coincide in a common vocation: *to radicalize mission*.

Radicalizing mission is what is peculiar to religious life, for mission in itself, in its different forms, is part of the vocation of every Christian. Even a full-time dedication to the apostolate is insufficient to identify the radicalism of the apostolate of religious, for there were always many lay persons who made some form of the apostolate their profession. The radicalism of the mission of religious life is not found so much in the time dedicated to mission but in the "style" of missionary work. Mission to the most difficult and abandoned areas; where the church is most challenged and needed; where persons have less hope or have substituted idols for all hope; the poorest and most abandoned (who run the risk of losing hope); the most distant and the most corrupt; the most difficult apostolates—that is the radical style of mission. This style is in continuity with the lifestyle of those who realize mission. Living only for God prepares them to announce the God of hope in the milieux least open to hope.

If we observe the charism of the founders of diverse religious traditions, we see that they habitually conceived of the apostolic objective of their foundation precisely in those terms. The diverse forms and reforms of religious life emerge in the history of the church as a response to new, unusual, and difficult pastoral situations, which imply great risk and generosity. When it is a question of reviving today the foundational charisms of religious institutes, it is important to recuperate the radicalism of their mission and ask oneself how the founders would have responded today to the new challenges faced by evangelization.

Hence, for example, *the preferential option for the poor* and oppressed, which constitutes at this time one of the factors of the renovation of religious life, is completely coherent with its missionary radicalism. The most poor and abandoned of the earth cannot be evangelized and liberated on the basis of purely human aspirations—whose realization no one can assure—or on the basis of substitutes for Christian hope. They can be evangelized and liberated only on the basis of the promise of God, lived in spite of misery and injustice as the dynamism of dignity, freedom, and hope.

Among the poor, the distant, and sinners, religious life will always have a significant role—to share with them their misery, aspirations, and searches, offering them by the witness of life not always a solution to all their desires and aspirations, but offering primarily the fundamental Christian experience: that the God of the promises is always faithful to them, and that in the midst of the lack of pleasure, power, and possessions, life has meaning because of hope.

10

The Prayer of Hope

I have covered all the themes that can help us with a spirituality of hope. But I have not referred explicitly to prayer, which is the axis of any spirituality, even though prayer, and more than anything an attitude of prayer, was in the background of these reflections, and even though it is a necessary condition for living Christian hope. Let me dedicate a word to the theme by way of synthesis and conclusion.

Together with the sacraments, the realization of our hope acquires its greatest intensity here on earth in our moments of prayer. Prayer in itself is *a prolonged act of hope*. Prayer, which is an exclusive and loving encounter with God, prepares us, little by little and by the dynamism of that love, for God's way of being. It prepares our being and our faculties for the permanent and definitive encounter with God. Therefore prayer anticipates for us and gives us a taste of the contents of the promise. For this reason the mystics consider prayer the place par excellence for the experience of God and God's gifts.

If spirituality, and particularly the spirit of hope, incite us to *live the present with love*, that is precisely what we do in prayer. We never dedicate ourselves to the present as absolutely as when we pray. Through profound intimacy and identification in love between God and ourselves created in prayer, we introduce ourselves in the "now" of prayer into the eternal "now" of God. For that reason, in some way or other, we transcend time and place in prayer and we can pray and have influence throughout the world and in all persons.

Hope is equally the certitude that God will give us the necessary means, always and in any circumstances of life, to realize and attain these promises. This is called confidence in providence. Prayer is not understood unless we have confidence that

God wants to save and liberate us, and remove from our path the obstacles to such promise, and that we can and should always ask for this in prayer, which God certainly hears and answers.

Prayer not only actualizes and deepens the practice of hope in an eminent way, it also *educates our hope*. It has been said that prayer, in secular judgment, appears to be a waste of time, an unrealistic search, a confidence without foundation. For many, these feelings generate other temptations about prayer. Because of this, praying, leaving behind every temptation to the contrary, always involves a risk, in the sense that faith and hope are always a risk for the unbeliever. The confidence and the courage of faith (the "risk") that we have when we pray comes from hope, and at the same time increases and strengthens the quality of our hope. The truth is that the more prayer is tempted, somber, arid, and unsatisfactory for our senses, the more we are educated for hope, which becomes more rooted in us.

We are also educated for hope by the fact that prayer is an eminent practice of gratuitous love. I said before that hope cannot arise in persons who are incapable of acting and loving gratuitously, without expecting a response, and who are incapable of forgetting their immediate interests.

In prayer we practice this form of gratuitousness as something inherent to it, although we are not aware of it. *Prayer is essentially gratuitous*, which does not exclude it from also being efficacious and having redeeming and liberating effects in humanity. Prayer remains essentially gratuitous because what we seek most in it is the experience of God's love, friendship, and plenitude. We seek to be with, adore, and praise God, because God is God, even when this brings us no apparent benefit. The more our attitude of gratuitousness in prayer grows—praying purely for the love of God—the more our hope is deepened. For on earth there is no true gratuitousness without true hope.

Prayer educates hope likewise by way of purification. *Prayer purifies* the impediments to hope by going to the center of our life "in the one thing necessary" (Luke 10:38–42). This experience in prayer, to the God who is given to us now, gradually relativizes and heals our relation with the past and the future. These cease to be so important, and we perceive that the one thing important is the reign of God and God's promise, to which we must bring and integrate our friendships, aspirations, and the orientation of our heart, our desire (Matt. 6:19–34): "Your heavenly Father knows all that you need. Seek first his kingship over you, his way of holiness, and all these things will be given you besides. Let tomorrow take care of itself. Today has troubles enough of its own." To pray is to experience the truth of these words, and their call to desire God as our only trustworthy hope.

Therefore prayer educates hope; it is the *privileged experience of the desire for God*, which simultaneously increases our "hunger and thirst," and incites us to seek him with more intensity. In sum, the spirit of prayer is the very desire for God. It is the way we learn to desire and look for him above all our own interests and desires, conforming them to the will of God, and to the rhythm and manner in which God realizes them.

This last point is of particular importance in the education and purification of hope. *In prayer we learn to wait*, to wait for the realization of our desire for God in the future life, to wait for the progressive anticipation of the promises of God in the present life, to wait for the hour of God and of God's grace, which God alone knows, to wait for God's answer to our petitions. Hope is purified by learning to wait.

The biblical insistence on constant, permanent prayer without intermission (e.g., Matt. 7:7–11; Luke 11:5–13) corresponds to the necessity that prayer have a dimension of confident waiting, for one persists in prayer when one waits for God to respond. God responds in God's ways and not ours. Praying in this way cultivates the daughter of hope, patience with history.

Lastly, we should not forget that prayer incorporates us into the very prayer of Christ, and identifies us progressively with his mode of praying. Through his prayer the humanity of Jesus expressed that his absolute love of the Father was present in each moment of his life; expressed his burning desire that the promise of God be fulfilled and that the reign come (Luke 11:2; John 4:23; Luke 12:49–50). Through his prayer, Jesus waited for his own death and the new and permanent life of the resurrection.

Although we do not yet enjoy the vision of the Father, we pray in hope. Hope brings us to pray in the same way as Christ — to desire the love of God in each present moment, to desire the realization of the promise and the reign of God in us and in all humanity, to wait for death as the passover from hope to the promise.